LINCOLN
RAMBLES

Countryside Books' walking guides cover most areas of England and include the following series:

County Rambles
Walks For Motorists
Exploring Long Distance Paths
Literary Walks
Pub Walks

A complete list is available from the publishers:

3 Catherine Road, Newbury, Berkshire

LINCOLNSHIRE RAMBLES

Seventeen Country Walks around Lincolnshire

Brett Collier

_____

With Historical Notes

COUNTRYSIDE BOOKS
NEWBURY, BERKSHIRE

COUNTRYSIDE BOOKS
3 Catherine Road
Newbury, Berkshire

ISBN 1 85306 226 X

Cover Photograph of Scamblesby
reproduced by kind permission
of Lincolnshire County Council

Produced through MRM Associates Ltd., Reading
Typeset by Acorn Bookwork, Salisbury
Printed in England by J. W. Arrowsmith Ltd., Bristol

Dedication

Dedicated to those stout-hearted walkers from Lincoln Group, Ramblers Association who acted as guinea pigs in attempting to follow my draft route instructions.

Contents

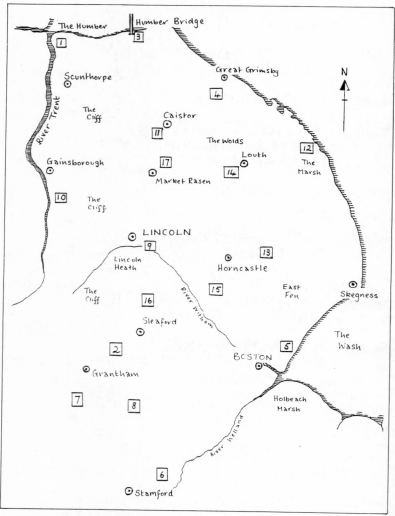

Area map showing the location of the walks.

Introduction

Lincolnshire stretches across a vast area from its former northern border on the Humber Bank down to the Wash. The 'old Lincolnshire' from the Humber to the Cambridgeshire border is a very large county indeed for there is a distance of about 80 miles between the Barton upon Humber walk and the one at Greatford, near Stamford. At the time of writing it appears likely that in the near future South Humberside will be reunited once again with Lincolnshire, hence its inclusion in these walks.

'Dull, flat, uninteresting . . .' people say who have never set foot in the county and while it is true that the fen and marsh lands of the south and east of the county are flat, the wide horizons and immense sky have a very special charm of their own and the area is known locally as Big Sky Country. Drainage of the fens was started by the Romans and continued by the monks to help create a rich, black peat soil, the most fertile soil in England. It is roughly 350 years since the area of Lincolnshire known as the Fens were redrained by Peter Vermuyden and his Dutch engineers. Today the Fens are often likened to Holland with its flat landscape, crisscrossed by drains and ditches with no stone walls and few hedges.

However, in contrast the landscape of the Lincolnshire Wolds is unique in its combination of dramatic western scarp, rolling chalk uplands with large arable fields, deepsided dry valleys with rich chalk grassland communities, farmsteads surrounded by mature shelter belts and unspoilt villages, much of which is designated as an Area of Outstanding Natural Beauty. Most of these Wold villages are sited in valleys as water was scarce on the hilltops. Until the Middle Ages there were many more villages than there are today, partly due to the ravages of the Black Death.

The Romans were here and left their mark on roads, towns, sea banks and dykes. After the Romans it formed the kingdom of Mercia until the Danish invasions and by AD 886 the whole county had become part of the Danelaw with two Danish Boroughs of Stamford and Lincoln. There really should have been a Stamfordshire. The 'by' and 'thorpe' endings of village names betray their Danish origin and they account for about a third of all the village names in the county, hence the evocatively named Viking Way long distance recreational path which is not a route taken by the Vikings but through territory they had made their own.

Although more accessible today, in the past Lincolnshire was almost an island. The long North Sea coast is without any real navigable rivers except for the indentation of the Humber and the Wash, while southwards the band of swamp and marsh merging with the Fen, plus the direct northward course of the river Trent, one of England's largest rivers, on its way from Newark to fall into the estuary of the Humber, have all contributed to its comparative geographical isolation.

No crowded or feet-eroded fieldpaths here, for one of the great attractions of Lincolnshire nowadays is that it is still possible to walk all day without meeting anyone, except in the villages or perhaps to wave to a tractor driver across an enormous field. All the walks are on public rights of way except for the very occasional permissive path.

Our public rights of way heritage in Lincolnshire, once the worst obstructed in England and Wales, is improving dramatically under the energetic administration of the Recreational Services Department of the County Council who rather belatedly have recognised the potential of countryside recreation now that farming policies no longer dominate the scene. Today there is even a Council official entitled the Principal Countryside Access Development Officer!

Parking should not be a problem but we would ask walkers to give every consideration to local inhabitants when parking and particularly not to obstruct field gates. It is a good habit to always try to leave the countryside better than you found it by picking up a piece of litter, for this helps to counter the argument that more walkers means more litter. Enjoy your walking in Lincolnshire and try to keep the Country Code whenever it is possible to do so.

Brett Collier
April 1993

COUNTRY CODE

1. Guard against all risks of fire.
2. Fasten all gates.
3. Keep dogs under proper control.
4. Keep to the paths across farmland.
5. Avoid damaging fences.
6. Leave no litter.
7. Safeguard water supplies.
8. Protect wild life, wild plants and trees.
9. Go carefully on country roads.
10. Respect the life of the countryside.

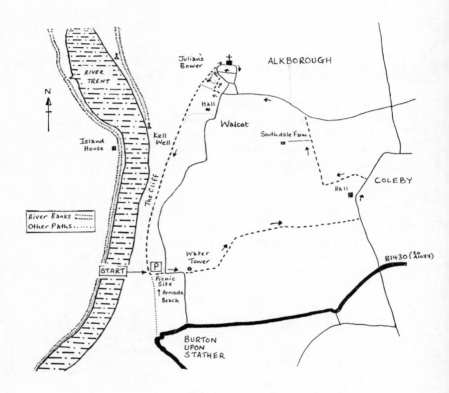

Alkborough
and The River Trent

Introduction: An attractive walk in relatively unknown countryside, even to locals, with splendid views over the Isle of Axholme and, on clear days, all the way to York Minster. At one point in the walk there is a distant view of the Humber Bridge. Alkborough itself is a pleasant village with a number of items of interest, including the 12th century maze at Julian's Bower.

Distance: 7 miles of easy walking almost entirely on good tracks, taking about four hours with time for a picnic lunch at Julian's Bower. OS Map Landranger Sheet 112 Scunthorpe.

Refreshments: None en route but The Sheffield Arms at Burton upon Stather does bar meals of an exceptionally high standard. At the time of writing there was one general store in Alkborough and several in Burton upon Stather.

Good parking at Burton upon Stather picnic site off the Alkborough road but there are no toilet facilities there or en route.

How to get there: Burton upon Stather is situated 5½ miles north of Scunthorpe. The starting place for the walk is the picnic site ¾ mile north of the village on a signposted scenic route to Alkborough near the prominent water tower (GR 870 187).

The walk: Walk back down the track to the road and follow the good track and signposted bridleway straight on past the water tower. Ignore the first track to the left but when opposite the wood on the right, some 500 yards beyond the tower, turn left on a clear track with the hedge on your immediate left. Continue on this track with the hedge on your left all the way to the road and Coleby village, ignoring another track leading to the left.

Turn left on the road into and through Coleby, to turn left off the road by the white barn at the far end of the village. Pass the farm buildings on the track and after 700 yards turn right by the telegraph pole (waymark) and continue forward on this good track down into the dip, following the line of poles. Walk straight forward at the top of the slope with Southdale Farm on the left and a splendid view of the Humber Bridge about 7 miles away on the right.

Walk on to the road and then turn left towards Alkborough for 1,200 yards and, at the sharp right-hand bend in the road, walk straight forward on the signposted footpath into College Close. Cross the Burton upon Stather to Alkborough road and almost directly opposite follow the signposted footpath for about 175 yards before turning right at the path junction on a waymarked path through the trees with the Roman encampment on the left.

Turn left at the road and continue along to the church and the remains of the ancient cross by the porch. On leaving the church grounds turn left up the wide Main Street and then right down Cross Lane back to Julian's Bower.

Turn right into Julian's Bower with its ancient maze and magnificent viewpoint overlooking the Isle of Axholme and the confluence of the Trent and the Ouse. From the viewpoint follow the good clifftop path for 2 miles back to the picnic site and your starting place.

Historical Notes

Kell Well is a remarkable spring, issuing from the cliff and overhung with trees, visited chiefly in days gone by for its hag-stones found in the channel, said to be similar to those carried by the ancients as amulets or lucky stones. Throughout East Anglia the hag-stone was the symbol of the eye, the hole representing the pupil; it is the equivalent of the All-Seeing Eye which has always been a powerful symbol all over the world and is still seen today on the prows of boats in the Mediterranean and the Far East. Egyptian traditions record that Horus, the son of Osiris fought with his uncle Set and lost an eye in combat which was restored by Thoth spitting upon it. The eye thus became a symbol of sacrifice and later a protection against evil influences.

Alkborough has traces of a large encampment near the northern termination of the lofty cliff, being the Aquis of Ravenas some 300 ft square, and the vallum or ditch may still be distinctly traced. It is a good defensive position guarding the confluence of two large rivers. The enclosure is called Countess Close from Countess Lucy, wife of Tailbois who, in the time of William the Conqueror, was Lord of Holland. At that time the whole manor of Alkborough belonged to Countess Lucy.

The Tudor Walcot Hall has some lovely gardens and magnificent trees. The present owners are said to have planted 1,000 trees in the last few years.

The maze at Julian's Bower, Alkborough is 44 ft across, cut into the turf and is believed to have been made in the 12th century by the monks of a cell established here from Spalding Priory. There is an explanatory plaque on site. On the floor of the church porch there is a replica in stone.

The remnant of an ancient cross near the church porch has been defaced through the centuries by sharpening scythes on the edges and the long cuts in the stone at the back are believed to have been made by sharpening arrow heads in the medieval period, when every region had to provide trained archers. There were butts at the end of the main street.

On the 29th December 1170 Thomas a Becket was murdered by four knights in his own cathedral of Canterbury. After committing the murder, Hugo Morville, William Tracy, Richard Brito and Reginald Fitzurse hid for a time in Yorkshire and then surrendered themselves to the Pope's Legate in England, who ordered them to take a pilgrimage to Jerusalem. However, none of them went, for Reginald Fitzurse sailed to Ireland and the other three turned up in Alkborough and rebuilt the church, presumably as an act of contrition.

Ancaster

Introduction: A pleasant walk across the Heath and over gently undulating countryside, beginning in the village of Ancaster, an important place in Roman times. The village stands on Ermine Street Roman road, known hereabouts as the High Dyke, and the first part of the walk leads one up an attractive dry valley and nature reserve that is reputed to have been used in the past for chariot races. The stone-built villages of Oasby, Aisby and Kelby are visited and the walk takes one by the lakes and through the grounds of 17th century Culverthorpe Hall.

Distance: 9 miles of fairly easy walking, much of it on good tracks but with some cross-field paths and, on the return section, innumerable stiles that at least make good waymarks. Say 4½ hours with time for refreshment at Oasby or a picnic lunch at a lake at Culverthorpe. Also a 4 mile alternative walk. OS Map Landranger Sheet 130 Grantham.

Refreshments: There is a general store in Ancaster Main Street. The Ermine Way public house, Ancaster (Tel: Lovenden 0400 30440) serves bar meals, as does the Houblon Arms Inn, Oasby (Tel: Culverthorpe 052 95 215). The Oasby Pot Shop (Tel: Culverthorpe 052 95 234) is a craft pottery shop and general store. Refreshments are available in the garden or conservatory.

How to get there: Take the A607 road from Grantham and then the A153 road to Sleaford, with Ancaster 7½ miles down this road from Grantham or 6 miles from Sleaford. Alternatively, take the Newark to Sleaford road A17(T), turning off at Byard's Leap for 3½ miles along the Ermine Street Roman road. Park in the long main street on the wide verge opposite the Ermine Way public house, by the entry into the village recreational field (GR 983 438).

The Walk: From your parking place walk down the Main Street towards the church and cross-roads. Turn left towards Sleaford, cross the busy road with care and walk up the right-hand grass verge for 100 yards. The hummocks over the stone wall in the field opposite mark the site of the Roman town.

Turn right on a signposted path and then go over the stile on the right into the nature reserve. The pleasant grass track on the left is your return route. Walk up the attractive valley for almost ¾ mile and bear left at the top to continue straight forward, with a hedge on the left and Valley Farm over on the right, as far as Heath Lane.

(It would be possible to have a much shorter walk by turning left along Heath Lane for 600 yards and then turning diagonally left across the field to walk along the top of the valley as outlined in the instructions for the return walk. This would provide a 4 mile walk.)

Cross Heath Lane and continue forward on a good track with the hedge now on your right and a glimpse of the spire of Heydour church ahead. Ignore public paths to the left and right and continue straight forward until at the end of the track you meet a signposted permissive path turning left for 200 yards to join the lane.

Turn right down the lane and at the T-junction walk straight ahead on a signposted path to a waymark, ditch-board and stile. In the next field turn diagonally right, aiming to the right of the large new house with the red roof. Cross another ditchboard and stile and then go diagonally left towards the new house and a metal kissing gate in the field corner. Go through the kissing gate and down the narrow passage to the village grass triangle with the Pot Shop and the Houblon Arms on the right.

After refreshment or a look around the village, retrace

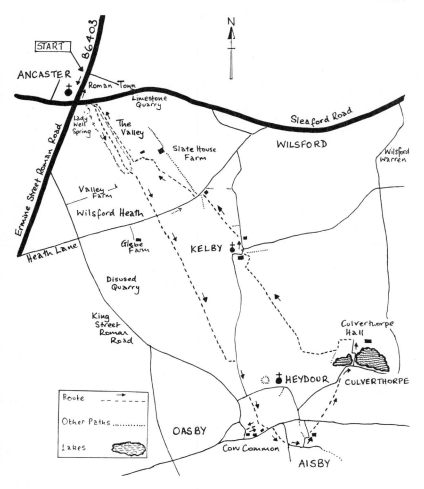

your steps along the narrow passage to the metal kissing gate and walk straight forward with the wooden stabling now on your immediate right. Turn left at the road for 120 yards and then right on a signposted path across Cow Common with the recreational field on your left. Cross over the road and follow the narrow lane round to the left passing Heydour Village Hall (in Aisby). Just beyond the large farm buildings

19

of Manor Farm on the right, turn right off the road on a signposted path to walk 300 yards diagonally left to a sign-post and stile in the hedge on the lane.

Go straight across the road to follow the same path across the next two fields, walking directly towards Culverthorpe Hall seen on the opposite slope. Turn right on the road for 350 yards round the bend to the drive leading to Culver-thorpe Hall. Walk up the driveway despite its misleading notice, for this is a public bridleway, to pause to have a look at or wander round the lakes with their large concentration of ducks and Canada geese. There is a picnic site by the side of the lake and display boards.

Continue your walk up the drive on the metalled track towards the farm buildings. Just beyond the wall and farm buildings turn left on a clear, signposted track and, at the end of the field follow the track round to the left for about 120 yards. Turn right on a signposted path and walk forward with the hedge on the left for the length of one field to the next hedge. Turn right here and walk along with the hedge on your immediate right. Ignore the path to the right and cross six fields until you approach Manor Farm at Kelby. The public right of way has been diverted around the farm buildings so bear to the right and then turn left just beyond the buildings into Kelby, towards the church. It is often muddy here with cattle. Climb the stile in the corner by the house and pond and turn left on the lane towards the church.

Turn right at the junction with the church on your left for 150 yards, ignoring the other lane on the right. Down in the dip turn off the road on a signposted path opposite some buildings and walk diagonally left uphill to the hedge T-junction. Go through the hedge and left across the field to a paddock and aim for the fieldgate in the corner with Heath House on your right. There is another path coming out onto the road over the hedge.

Go diagonally right across the road where there are again two paths – one leading up the track to Slate House Farm and the other, which is the one you need to follow, diagon-ally left across the field. It should be clearly defined. Walk almost as far as the old buildings behind Slate House Farm and then bear left to join a good track on the top of the ridge above the valley. Turn right on this pleasant path all the way to the road. Turn left on the main road, cross with care, and walk right up Ancaster Main Street to your starting place.

Historical Notes

Ancaster was an important Roman station ('castra' meaning camp) for it was the last staging post on Ermine Street before Lincoln was reached. It is believed to have been the Roman Causen-nae. The camp covers nine acres and it is seen at its best at the start of the walk at the corner opposite the church. Thousands of coins have been found here, 2,000 of them in one spot, and many Ancaster folk traded Roman coins in the 18th century. Grantham Museum has a number of exhibits gathered from the Ancaster area; a small altar, a milestone, Roman sculpture and other artifacts.

Ancaster has given its name to the stone which has built many of our old churches and modern buildings, for the limestone has a special quality of hardening after exposure.

Just down the road commanding the Ancaster Gap is the hill fort of Honington, that is also situated on the great prehistoric Jurassic ridgeway that ran from the south-west of Britain on into Yorkshire. From Honington it follows the scarp edge into Lincoln. These Iron Age farmers around 250 BC were the forerunners of the people later known as the Coritani.

Culverthorpe: There have been settlements in other parts of the area since at least Anglo-Saxon times and Culverthorpe would have been an outlying settlement of Heydour. Culverthorpe had a church in 1086 but not in 1992; actually, Culverthorpe means a place of worship.

Land enclosure began in the 17th century when sheep rearing became important. The final enclosure of the remaining heath and common land did not take place until 1803. In 1981 the population of the three villages of Kelby,

Culverthorpe and Heydour at 300 was just half of what it was a hundred years earlier.

The present hall at Culverthorpe dates from the 17th century although there was an earlier house on the site. In the early 1600s Culverthorpe Hall was bought by the Newtons, relatives of Sir Issac's family who lived at Woolsthorpe. Newtons are buried in Heydour church. Sir John Newton died in 1734, followed three years later by his wife. Their son, Sir Michael Newton only survived his father by eight years and his only son died in tragic circumstances. When he was a three month old baby he was stolen by a pet monkey and in the panic of pursuit thrown to his death from the roof of Sir Michael's London apartment. The house later passed to the Archer Houblon family, hence the name of the inn at Oasby.

Heydour stands between the source of three rivulets and its name comes from 'dour' – water and 'hay' – enclosure. In the field west of the church are traces of the moat of a castle believed to have been built in the 12th century.

Barton Upon Humber and The Humber Bridge

Introduction: An easy but fascinating riverside walk near an ancient town dominated by the superb grace of the modern bridge. Waterbirds may be observed on the many lakes of the former clay pits and perhaps some river traffic proceeding to and from the small ports upstream. It is a birdwatcher's paradise and a place of national ornithological importance, with the majority of the pits scheduled as Sites of Special Scientific Interest.

Distance: 4 miles of easy walking mainly on good tracks, making it a leisurely ramble of under two hours. OS Map Landranger Sheet 112 Scunthorpe.

Refreshments: None en route but you must pass The Sloop Inn, Waterside on the way to and from the Viewing Area. At the time of writing the refreshment kiosk at the Viewing Area had not been taken for the summer season.

At the Viewing Area Car Park there are toilets, picnic tables and an Information Centre for Barton Clay Pits in The Old Boat House. There is an hourly bus service across the bridge to Hull.

How to get there: Going northwards from Brigg or Scunthorpe all roads lead to the bridge but take care to turn off the motorway for Barton upon Humber town before you are actually committed to the bridge crossing. The Humber Bridge Viewing Area is signposted throughout the town but beware of the one-way system. Travelling southwards over

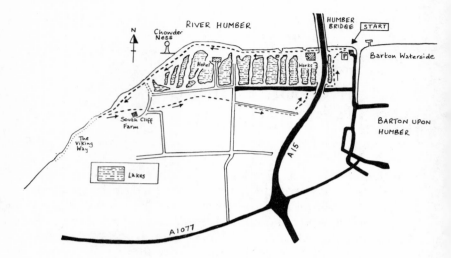

the bridge you simply turn left off the road into Barton upon Humber town at the first exit. (GR 028 234.)

The walk: From the top of the embankment overlooking the river Humber walk upstream towards the bridge on a good track past the William Blyth tileworks, the Barton Outdoor Pursuits Centre for Youth Service Groups with an enormous beached barge outside, Westfield Lakes Caravan Park and Hotel and Far Ings Nature Reserve. Continue along the embankment through the metal kissing gate, past the small jetty to Chowder Ness navigation marker, with an opportunity here for an apple stop.

About 1,000 yards beyond the navigation marker turn left off the embankment down the wooden steps to the foot-bridge and stile on a signposted public footpath, to walk towards the bridge and along the field edge to South Cliff Farm. The correct route goes in front of the farmhouse but it has been waymarked on the farm track behind the farmhouse and it is understood the route is under negotiation for a diversion application. Turn left on the farm track and a few yards beyond the bend turn right off the track on a signposted footpath and stile. Continue with the hedge on the right around the small copse to a stout footbridge over a dyke and then across the field to the metal fieldgate in the right-hand corner.

Cross Gravel Pit Lane and walk straight forward along the metalled track known as Dam Road (now cut by the bridge embankment) with allotments and a deep ditch on your right. At the road end turn left along the attractive meandering path with bark chippings underfoot marked Woodland Path, courtesy of the Bridge Board.

On reaching the road turn right under the bridge and walk along Far Ings Road and, after 175 yards, turn left off the road on a good grass track into the Barton Clay Pits and on to the car park and viewpoint.

Historical Notes

Barton is a place of great antiquity and was once surrounded by a rampart and a fosse, traces of which may still be seen at Castle Dykes. At the Norman Conquest it was a corporate town with a reeve, aldermen, etc. It was once the biggest port on the Humber until Hull grew and took away its old importance, leaving it a little market town by the waterside.

Barton's St Peter's church, known locally as Old St Peter's, has a Saxon tower that is one of the most remarkable examples of Saxon architecture in all England.

The river Humber: The Viewpoint is the start of the 140 mile long Viking Way, a long distance recreational path that leads through South Humberside, across Lincolnshire and through Rutland, Leicestershire to end at Oakham. The Humber Bank walk is also part of the route of the Nev Cole Way starting at Barton upon Stather and ending, after 67 miles of interesting walking, at Nettleton, near Caistor, Lincolnshire. There is an exhilarating walkway over the bridge which is the connecting link between The Wolds Way Path and the Viking Way.

The magnificent bridge across the river Humber com-

25

pletely dominates the walk for it is the longest single span suspension bridge in the world with a main span of 4,626 ft. The total length between anchorages is 7,284 ft (1.38 miles or 0.86 kilometres) and the clearance over the water is 98 ft.

The Country Park and Nature Reserve: The series of lakes beside the path are old flooded clay workings that are being developed into a linear Country Park that stretches over 5 miles. The task of the Countryside Project Officer is to achieve a balance between recreational needs such as yachting, wind-surfing, fishing and canoeing and the wildlife conservation of this unique area.

Along this low-lying plain next to the Humber the extensive man-made workings form the largest area of freshwater marsh in the region. Their varying depths have created a mixture of dense reed beds and open waters bordered by scrub woodland and grassland, all of which supports a variety of wild life. Because of their conservation importance the majority of the pits are scheduled as Sites of Special Scientific Interest.

The Far Ings Reserve has five viewing hides, shallow and deep water areas, reedbeds, woodland and well maintained pathways. Visitors are welcome but they are asked to keep to the paths and to allow no dogs onto the reserve.

Reed mace, water forget-me-not, brooklime, water plantain and fools watercress may be seen, with celery leafed buttercup and wild celery, at Far Ings. Quite a lot of alders have been planted for they are not found as a wild tree in this area. One of the major features of the Clay Pits are the magnificent old hawthorn hedges which thrive on the heavy clay.

In the past five years the Clay Pits area has gained a few new breeding species of birds such as the greylag goose, ruddy duck and possibly the sparrowhawk. Collared doves, lesser whitethroats and Canada geese have increased while birds such as the bearded tit, common whitethroat, red poll and mute swan are now low in numbers.

Bradley Woods

Introduction: A pleasant walk over level ground through quiet countryside, woods and farmland, beginning in the attractive 62 acre Bradley Woods owned by Great Grimsby Borough Council. The woods themselves are a delightful area to explore with their own picnic and play area and on the walk there are pleasant villages, beck-side paths and fine, open views. Although not dramatic it is quite different from the Wolds, the Heath or the Fen, for this region is a peaceful and undiscovered area for very many people that perhaps unexpectedly really adds something to the variety of Lincolnshire walks on offer. Actually it isn't in Lincolnshire today but it is confidently anticipated that South Humberside will return to Lincolnshire once more.

Distance: 7½ miles mainly on good tracks and headland paths, taking around 4 hours with a refreshment stop. OS Map Landranger Sheet 113 Grimsby.

Refreshments: The Ship Inn, Barnoldby le Beck (Tel: Grimsby 0472 822 308) serves bar meals, but is closed on Mondays. There is a picnic site at Laceby Beck. The Nag's Head, The Square, Laceby (Tel: Grimsby 0472 74961) also serves bar meals and is open weekdays 11 am to 11 pm. Laceby has some general stores, including a Chinese takeaway.

How to get there: On the A46 Lincoln to Grimsby road, turn at the Laceby roundabout onto the A18 and at the Bradley roundabout leave the main road to turn into Bradley village. Bradley Woods are just through the village. Alternatively turn onto the A18 Louth road at Laceby roundabout and take the first left to Barnoldby le Beck and the first left again to Bradley Woods (GR 244 059).

The walk: From the car park in Bradley Woods have a look at the Wanderlust Rambling Club's display board to the late Nev Cole, a founder member. A 20 mile circular walk has been created in his name starting from this spot.

Turn left from the display board along a signposted bridleway on a good track and, at the wood edge, continue straight forward with the hedge on your left. Cross the track to Low Farm and continue forward towards Barnoldby le Beck, crossing Team Gate Drain with Glebe Farm Cottage on the left. Have a look at the obelisk by the church and then proceed along Church Lane to the main road.

Turn right at the road for about 170 yards and right again on a signposted track for almost 1½ miles towards Manor

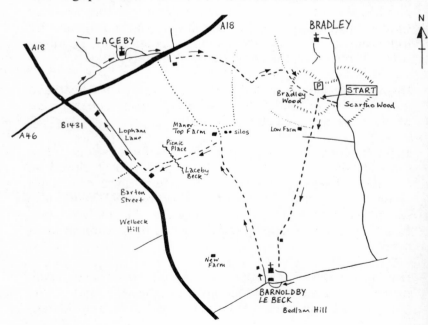

Top Farm. Turn left on a signposted path by the new golf course just before you reach Manor Top Farm, down to Laceby Beck and picnic site and then on to the pleasant green lane, known as Lopham Lane. Avoid the bridge over the ditch on the left but follow the lane that eventually becomes a metalled road until you reach the A18. Cross the busy main road with care, into Caistor Road which leads you into the square near the church and The Nag's Head.

Walk down Grimsby Road until you come to the main road once again. Cross the dual carriageway and enter the driveway of The Limes where there is a footpath signpost. Turn left through a wooden gate in front of the house and walk across to the far right-hand corner of the field where there is a metal gate. Keep the hedge on your immediate right through the next field to reach a stile and bridge over a dyke. Continue forward with the ditch on the right, crossing a farm track and stile until the path bends to the left and another bridge.

Turn right and cross over into the next field with Bradley Woods over on your right. Continue to follow the path with the ditch on your right until you meet a wide, grassy cross-track. Turn right here until you reach the edge of the wood and then left to follow the path until you reach the white house situated at the corner of the wood. Turn right into the wood on the bridlepath and, after some 200 yards take any path to the right which leads you to the play area, the main drive and your starting place.

Historical Notes

Bradley is a charming village with the small Norman church of St George and a lovely brick creeper-clad manor house built in 1689.

Barnoldby le Beck looks over the flat land to the Humber some 5 miles away. A granite column by the churchyard gate marks the spot where William Smith, the Huntsman for the Earl of Yarborough, was thrown from his horse and received injuries from which he died.

Laceby is a big village just off the main road to Grimsby and it has an old church built towards the end of the Norman period and a rector who won fame throughout the land. He was the fearless John Whitgift, born in 1530, who became Elizabeth I's Archbishop of Canterbury and lived to place the crown upon the head of James I. The church registers date from 1538, the year that Thomas Cromwell made their keeping compulsory, and an entry in 1546 tells of the execution of a witch who was 'devoured' by fire.

Evidence of round barrows from prehistoric Britain may be traced in the area and Anglo-Saxon occupation sites have been found. The Romans were here and its nearness to the sea and a navigable river meant that the Danes made this land their own. Remnants of the old ridge and furrow farming from the medieval period can occasionally be found.

Freiston Shore

Introduction: An easy and atmospheric walk on good paths mainly along the top of both old and very recent sea banks, that is well worth the journey to this remote, wind-swept corner of Lincolnshire. These marshes were once the haunt of smugglers when the Wash came up close to the Bank and tales of hobgoblins and shagfoals on lonely roads in these parts were put about by smugglers to deter too curious inhabitants from reporting any strange, unlawful goings-on. Today the wealth of the reclaimed marsh lies in vegetables rather than contraband but the strangeness of the area remains with the two forlorn, derelict hotels and the end of a dream for a flourishing seaside resort. It is a different world here on this flat coastal edge overlooking the Wash with its immense sky and views across the Fen to Boston Stump, which for centuries has been a landmark for travellers across the Fen or for ships sailing along the coast.

Distance: Almost 4 miles of good walking on firm tracks taking about two hours if, with the help of binoculars, you wish to identify birds on the marsh or look at shipping lying offshore in Boston Deeps. OS Map Landranger 131 Boston and Spalding.

Refreshments: There are no refreshments on the walk, but to get to Freiston Shore one must pass through Freiston with The Bull and Dog, which serves bar meals (0205 760 403). The pub lies directly opposite the church where one must turn to get to Freiston Shore.

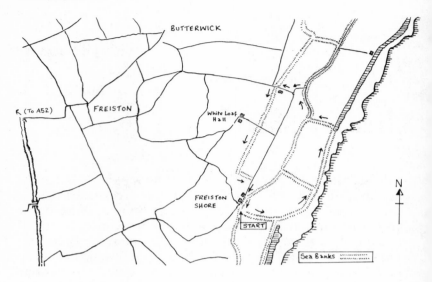

How to get there: Take the A52 Skegness road out of Boston and turn right to Freiston ¼ mile after crossing the Hobholes Drain. From Freiston follow the Shore Road, leaving Freiston church on your right, and on to Freiston Shore 2 miles away. It is signposted. At Freiston Shore park carefully on the grass off the road by the telephone kiosk, for enormous lorries use these narrow lanes to collect cabbages and other vegetables for market. (GR 398 424).

The walk: From your parking place go through the kissing gate on the signposted path and then straight ahead towards the sea along a good vehicular track with a new bank on your right.

At the end turn left along the top of the new sea bank for just over a mile and then left again down the slope either on the track itself or along the top of the bank on the right. Cross the vehicular track at the end to climb the stile and turn right for about 350 yards on the top of an older sea bank. Turn left at the road with the remains of an old machine gun post ahead and follow the road round to the right towards the white house named 'Chimnies' situated alongside an even older sea bank; do not take the road on the left leading directly back to Freiston Shore. Turn left off the road by 'Chimnies' on the signposted path along the sea bank with the dyke on your immediate right. White Loaf Hall is over on the right.

Continue along this bank and follow it round to the left until you meet the road. Turn right at the road for about 400 yards and then left up the bank on the signposted path along the top of the bank with the derelict Marine Hotel, now in a dangerous condition, on your right. Turn right at the stile back to your starting place.

Historical Notes

Freiston: The name came from a colony of Frielanders who settled on this spot, where today a large village has grown up between the Hobholes Drain and the sea. Once the sea came up to it but today it is 2 miles from Freiston Shore and the sea is still receding as new banks are built, leaving the old mud flats with a carpet of sand grasses and wild flowers washed only by the highest tides.

The local place name endings of -ton, -toft and -wick indicate Anglo-Saxon origins with strong Danish connections. In the Domesday Book there is ample evidence of a flourishing economy supporting a large population with more than the normal number of 'sokemen' or freemen and two churches were recorded, one of which would be Butterwick and the other Freiston.

St James Priory, a Benedictine foundation, was established at Freiston in 1114 by Alan de Creon, the son of the Norman baron Guy who came over with William the Conqueror. The priory later became a cell of Crowland Abbey and the glorious church of today is the remnant of the one that belonged to the priory. The inn called The Bull and Dog is said to have once been the guest house of the priory where important visitors were lodged.

Freiston church is a magnificent building with massive

12th century pillars and Norman arches. At the west end stands the 15th century octagonal font with part of the fastenings used to lock down the cover. Baptismal water was only consecrated once a year at Easter, so by order in 1236 all fonts had to be covered and locked to prevent witches stealing holy water.

The wildness of the marsh has been tamed by the construction of sea banks, a practice that began with the Romans and continues to the present day through the labours of the inmates of North Sea Camp, an Open Prison. Freiston Shore was destined to be the holiday resort of the Lincolnshire coast but the building of a railway direct to Skegness meant its rapid development and the subsequent decline of Freiston Shore. At one time there used to be horse racing here on the reclaimed flats above the tidal marsh and the two hotels, Plummers and the Marine had large windows on the seaward side to enable people to watch the racing from the comfort of their chairs. The Marine is now a dangerous ruin and Plummers ceased trading about a year ago, although the mews have been made into a number of quite attractive dwellings.

White Loaf Hall near the old sea bank has on one of its two stepped gables a stone shaped like a loaf, dated 1614. The first white loaf ever baked in England was made at this house, for until then brown bread had always been the staple diet. The house was a haunt for smugglers.

In 1711 John Linton became vicar at Butterwick and he resided at White Loaf Hall, from which a path led to his church. The third John Linton bought Freiston Priory in 1782 and he reclaimed much of the foreshore. When his orchard was repeatedly robbed of fruit, as a deterrent he set up a man-trap with a human leg in it that he had obtained from a surgeon. His fruit was left intact from then onwards!

Greatford

Introduction: Greatford is a charming village almost on the county boundary with the West Glen river flowing through the gardens of the Elizabethan hall and past the grey stone cottages. At one time the village was renowned for its watercress beds that are still shown on Ordnance Survey maps. This walk takes one across open fields, through woodland, alongside the river and into Braceborough, another ancient village where a Roman coffin was discovered in AD 350, for both villages are not far from the great Roman road known as King Street.

Distance: 4 miles of level walking mainly on good paths but with some cross-field paths that were defined at the time of writing. The walk should take something over two hours with time to look in the church and possibly a stop for refreshment. OS Map Landranger Sheet 142 Peterborough.

Refreshments: The Hare and Hounds, Greatford (Tel: 0788 560 332) serves bar food.

How to get there: Following the A15 Market Deeping to Bourne road turn westwards either at Baston or Langtoft across King Street Roman road to Greatford or, on the A6121 Stamford to Bourne road turn eastwards to Greatford near Carlby, which is 5 miles from Stamford or Bourne.

In Greatford pass the Hare and Hounds on the left and the church and hall on the right to park carefully on the grass verge at the entrance to the estate drive of Shillingthorpe Park estate, which is ½ mile beyond the hall or ½ mile before the railway crossing (GR 075 111).

The walk: Cross the stile to walk up the drive into Shilling-thorpe Park and over the West Glen river bridge. Ignore the first stile on the right and some 500 yards from the bridge and not far beyond the first stile, turn right at the signposted second stile. Cross the ditch and proceed diagonally right aiming to the right of the large tree in the field corner, where there is a stile and post with Braceborough church spire visible beyond.

Walk across the field on the defined path almost to the far left corner where there is a footbridge. Cross the bridge and turn left into the next field corner where there is a waymark. Turn right along the hedge and the ancient fallen trees to follow the waymark to the left along a good grass track to the road junction signposted 'Bracebor'. Walk down the lane towards the village with a thatched cottage on the right and a 'village green' on the left.

Turn right into the lane signed 'Church. No through road' with Braceborough Hall on the left. Just beyond the hall turn right up the metalled track at the edge of the village for 100 yards to walk straight on with The Gallery on your left and the stone well on the right. Go through the wooden fieldgate by the well and on across the paddock through a broken gate and on to a stile and a home-made wooden footpath signpost.

Walk straight across the arable field towards the large house in the trees, over a footbridge with a white handrail, to turn right along the field edge. Turn left at the field end towards Greatford church.

At the road walk straight forward into the village as far as the bridge over the West Glen river. Before crossing the bridge turn right through the white kissing gate down the church path with the river on your left and through the well-kept churchyard to the beautiful church.

From the church porch walk straight forward with the lovely Elizabethan Greatford Hall and its gardens on the right, cross the bridge over the river and turn left at the road to The Hare and Hounds and a welcoming landlord.

On leaving The Hare and Hounds turn right for a few

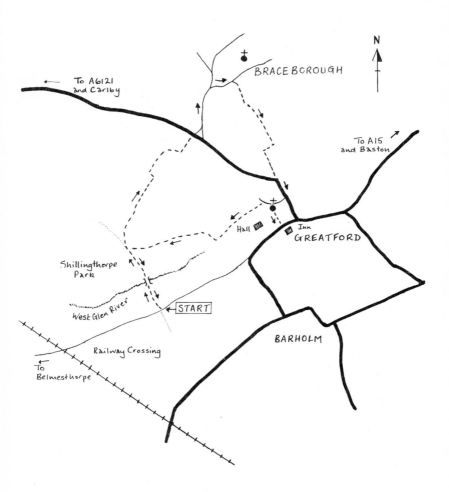

yards to the T-junction and then turn left with the old school on your right. Turn left up Greatford Gardens until you reach the iron gates of the estate and then turn right on the diverted signposted path at the bottom of someone's garden. Cross the footbridge and bear left on the waymarked path through the wood.

Over the stile, follow the edge of the field for 200 yards with a dyke and trees on the left. Turn left into the field to walk diagonally right across the field with the pond on your immediate left, to an earth bridge across the dyke and a waymark. Cross the next field, aiming to the right of the three old trees where you will find a stile. In the next small paddock walk diagonally right to a stile in the field corner. After crossing the stile turn left along the estate track back to the road that you used on the way out and where your car is parked.

Historical Notes

Braceborough, in a commanding position overlooking the Fen, was a beacon place to warn fen-dwellers of danger. It is recorded in the Domesday Book in 1086. At one time it boasted its own spa where water was bottled and sold. George III was rumoured to have taken the water when he was treated by Francis Willis who resided at Braceborough Hall. The three pre-enclosure farms, Ivy Farm, Manor Farm and Berry Farm still exist in the village centre.

The village hall was once the school and was built by the Willis family in 1870 and left in trust 'to be used for the education of adults and children of the labouring, manufacturing and other poorer classes in the parish of Braceborough.'

Greatford on the edge of the Great Marsh has a beautiful, stone-roofed mainly 13th century church with interesting monuments. One is to Francis Willis, MD, son of a clergyman of Lincoln cathedral who, in spite of family opposition, qualified as a doctor and helped found and conduct Lincoln Hospital to specialize in the treatment of insanity. He ran a private asylum for the mentally ill at Shillingthorpe. He cured George III of his first fit of madness and later his sons attended the king a second time but could not stave off the final breakdown. He became Vice-Principal of Brazenose College, Oxford and died in the 90th year of his age.

Another monument is dedicated to the Dowsetts of Great-ford Hall and there is a huge medieval gravestone enriched with a cross.

At one time Greatford was renowned for its watercress beds and they are still shown on current Ordnance Survey maps. There are some curious ornaments and an odd cross in the main street by The Hare and Hounds.

Harlaxton and Sewstern Lane

Introduction: A very varied walk through attractive countryside on the towpath of the disused Grantham Canal,
along the pre-Roman Sewstern Lane, through Denton
village, built mainly with the warm, golden local ironstone,
and around Denton reservoir, one of the two main feeder
reservoirs for the canal that is so popular with birdwatchers.

Distance: 8 miles of easy walking, but there may be muddy
sections. OS Map Landranger Sheet 130 Grantham.

Refreshments: Bar meals are available at the Welby Arms,
Denton (Tel: Grantham 0476 870304).

How to get there: Turn off the A1 road just south of
Grantham onto the A607 towards Melton Mowbray and
Harlaxton. Turn right off the A607 at Harlaxton crossroads
down The Drift almost as far as Harlaxton Bridge over the
Grantham Canal. Park on the wide, grass verge on the right
by Harlaxton Pumping Station, making sure to leave the
entrance clear (GR 882 335).

The walk: On leaving the car turn right down the road
towards Harlaxton Bridge over the Grantham-Nottingham
Canal. Cross the bridge and turn left down the steps onto the
towpath to walk forward with the canal on your left.
   Continue past Denton Wharf Bridge and Casthorpe
Bridge (about one hour) to turn left over the canal on the
concrete bridleway bridge and uphill on the clearly defined
path to a kissing gate. Cross the line of the disused mineral
railway to continue uphill and turn left near the top on

joining the green lane – a section of the Viking Way long distance recreational path.

Walk along this attractive green lane for about ¾ mile to cross the main road at Brewer's Grave and take the sign-posted Sewstern Lane bridleway marked with Viking Way waymarks, with the disused entrance to Belvoir Castle on the right.

Continue along Sewstern Lane for just over a mile until you reach Harston Road. Cross the road to turn almost immediately left into the steep, overgrown coppice and then walk along the field edge immediately below the road leading to Denton. After about 1,000 yards upon reaching the fence, climb the stile and regain the road to continue, in the same direction, into Denton village.

Turn right off the road by the distinctive Welby Arms sign

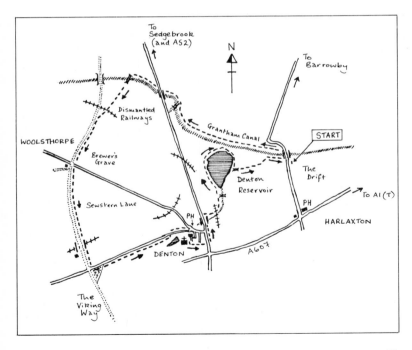

for liquid refreshment or bar food. On leaving The Welby Arms, by the front door turn right towards the church and then left on the signposted footpath opposite the church entrance path. Go through two kissing gates and then right up the lane for a few yards and left through another kissing gate along a signposted path.

On reaching the road cross to the opposite pavement and turn left downhill with the old post office and a telephone kiosk on the right. At the road bend and junction take the right-hand fork signposted Denton Wharf. After a couple of hundred yards, at the dip in the road turn right through a metal fieldgate along a good path with the stream on your immediate right. At the bridge continue straight forward over a stile until you reach Denton reservoir.

At the reservoir you may turn left or right but the left-hand route is particularly pleasant although slightly longer. On the left-hand route, ignore the good track down the embankment leading to a white gate to continue further around the reservoir path. Turn left (or right if you have done the shorter route) down the steps on the signposted path over the wooden bridge. Go straight forward with the hedge on your right at first and then through a wide gap in the hedge in front towards the canal bank, now on your immediate left, until you reach The Drift once again. Over the stile, turn right back to your starting place.

Historical Notes

Harlaxton Manor: The walk itself does not take you past the manor but you must pass it after turning off the A1 road and you will be able to see the quite extraordinary Jacobean-style building designed in 1830 that took 25 years to build. Today it is the European campus of the University of Evansville, Indiana.

Denton Reservoir: The reservoir is one of the two main feeder reservoirs for the Grantham Canal and pike, bream, roach and perch are caught here. You will probably see coot, moorhen, mallard, teal, heron and great crested grebe or even a kingfisher.

Grantham Canal: The Grantham to Nottingham Canal was 33 miles in length and rose nearly 140 ft to Grantham by a series of 18 locks. The main engineering features were the cutting at Harlaxton, this being 22 ft deep for a length of a mile, and the Denton Reservoir of 27 acres and that at Knipton of 52 acres. It was opened in 1799 and operated until 1936 when road and rail competition finally forced it to be abandoned. Within sight of Casthorpe Bridge you will see a milestone indicating that it is 30 miles to the river Trent. The County Council picnic site at Denton Wharf is a good apple stop. Iron-ore was carried on the canal from Brewer's Grave until that trade too fell to the railway.

Sewstern Lane is a prehistoric route far older than the neighbouring Roman roads. It ran from the Welland Valley (and perhaps from central East Anglia) to the river crossing at Newark and to other places in the Midland Plain. This drift road was used throughout the Middle Ages as a route between the great fairs of Nottingham and Stamford and later to connect the court at Belvoir Castle with the Royal Court in London. With the advent of public coaches and turnpike roads in the 17th century the old way fell out of use as it passes through no villages from Stamford to Long Bennington.

The Drift is a reference to its importance as a drove road in the past.

Brewer's Grave is reputed to have originated from a servant of the castle who drowned in a vat of ale.

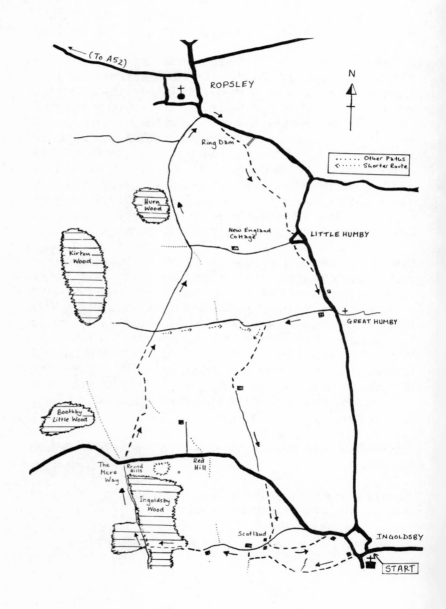

N

(To A52)

ROPSLEY

Ring Dam

Hurn Wood

Kirton Wood

New England Cottage

LITTLE HUMBY

GREAT HUMBY

Boothby Little Wood

The Mere Way

Round Hills

Red Hill

Ingoldsby Wood

Scotland

INGOLDSBY

START

······· Other Paths
<······ Shorter Route

Ingoldsby and The Mere Way

Introduction: This walk passes through peaceful woodland and along some splendid green lanes where deer and badger find food and shelter and many kinds of birds nest in the older woodland.

The Mere Way is a very ancient trackway that may have been some kind of tribal frontier and in Ingoldsby Woods is a circular encampment 500 ft in diameter called the Round Hills, that includes several tumuli. However, the leading Lincolnshire authority on prehistoric Lincolnshire is hesitant with regard to its date or purpose. From Ropsley, birthplace of a Tudor bishop and statesman, the walk returns through the villages of Great and Little Humby.

Distance: An 8 mile walk taking about four hours with a stop for refreshment. There is a shorter version of 5 miles for anyone whose time is limited.

Refreshments: The Green Man at Ropsley serves bar food (Tel: 047 685 223).

How to get there: Ingoldsby is 6 miles east of Grantham. Turn west off the A15 Sleaford to Bourne road by the Old Greyhound Inn, Folkingham on a B-road signed Ingoldsby for 5 miles, or off the Ancaster Roman road (The High Dyke) B6403 at the Grantham roundabout to follow the winding B1176 through undulating countryside for 6 miles via Old Somersby, Boothby Pagnell to Ingoldsby. Park carefully near the church entrance (GR 010301).

The walk: Walk down to the T-junction with the church on your left, to a signposted path by a metal fieldgate just across the road on the right. Walk straight across the rough pasture to the stile for the right-hand footpath. Walk down the valley on the clear reinstated path to a broken concrete bridge over the stream. Cross to walk up the other side of the valley and, at the top, bear left to a good track along the field boundary. Turn right here up to Scotland Lane towards the farmhouse with curiously shaped trees at the entrance. Turn left up Scotland Lane towards the wood, past the house on the left, under the vehicle bar, past the pond on the left to the wood itself. Walk alongside the wood edge for 100 yards and just before the dip in the track turn right into the wood on the waymarked path onto a wide ride. Continue on this ride for about 500 yards, ignoring junctions to left and right. Turn right on reaching The Mere Way, which is a good track becoming properly surfaced a little further on, and stay on this track until you reach the road.

Cross the road and take the right-hand green lane, for both tracks are only a few yards apart. Follow this attractive, ever-widening green lane around various bends for about ¾ mile until you come to the signposted track junction.

Turn right here for *the shorter route* although it is unsignposted as a public right of way because it is a county maintainable road. Continue along this surfaced track for about 1,100 yards and shortly after the second sharp bend you come to the signposted public footpath on the right. This cross-field path is the place you rejoin the longer route (see below).

For the longer route continue straight forward on this very wide lane for about 1¼ miles to Ropsley, ignoring any junctions to left or right and with New England Cottage away over on the right. On reaching the road junction, cross the road to The Green Man.

Turn left out of The Green Man along the High Street, becoming Humby Road, past the village store and post office. Some 60 yards beyond the 30 mph sign turn right over the stile on the signposted path and then left along the narrow tree-lined passage at the end of the house terrace. After the stile, cross the paddock to a footbridge and step stile and then two others. In the field corner on the left there is yet another footbridge, step stile and sign. Walk forward 20 yards and then turn right over the bridge to follow the right-hand edge of the field with the dyke on the immediate right all the way to the right-hand corner of the field. Climb the stile and continue forward some 120 yards to a further stile on the right. Cross and then turn left down the lane to Little Humby.

Cross the little green to the right towards the newly built house and, if the path is signposted, follow the public right of way and waymarks for about ¼ mile up to the lane. If it is not signposted walk up the lane, taking particular care on the bend for some 1,200 yards to Great Humby, passing the Great Northern Railway memorabilia in the garden of the house on the left.

Turn right off the road at Great Humby up the unsignposted county maintainable road leading to Humby Hall and continue forward on this vehicular track for about 700 yards, passing a small plantation on the left. Turn left off this track on a signposted path (*this is where the shorter route joins*) to cross the field diagonally right into the field corner where there is a bridge. Cross the farm bridge and proceed diagonally right to the hedge line. On reaching the hedge cross to the other side and turn left with the hedge on your immediate left. When the hedge turns, cross to the farm buildings and follow the good track all the way down to the road.

Cross the road and take the signposted footpath almost immediately opposite and walk straight forward into the dip on the reinstated path. In the second field aim towards the house on the right and in the corner you will find a stile leading into the garden and only a couple of yards away a second stile onto the lane.

Turn right on Scotland Lane for only a few yards and then left over a stile to proceed down the field towards the left-hand corner. Cross the small ford and walk diagonally left to another stile some 50 yards below the house on the road.

Turn right at the road and at the Ingoldsby road junction briefly left and then down Back Lane to your starting place.

Historical Notes

Ingoldsby: Before the Christian era water was the principal element of adoration or fear amongst the tribes in the area and as the village stands near the fork of two streams the inhabitants, who were water worshippers, named the place Ingodsby. Monks later altered the original name because of its pagan connections. The village has no association with the Ingoldsby Legends of Richard Barham.

Scotland: 'Scot' simply means payment for holding land.

Humby: This means a hump or hill.

Ropsley: In the village of Ropsley as late as 1937 there were two bakers, two shopkeepers, two grocers, a miller, motor engineer, dairyman, physician, wheelwright, joiner, saddler, tailor, bootmaker and three butchers all trading. One shop now remains and only a handful of people work from the village on the five local farms.

It is the birthplace of Richard Fox, Tudor bishop and statesman who was born in 1448 at the Peacock Inn, now a stone cottage that still stands on the High Street. He died at the age of 80 in 1528 and was laid to rest in his cathedral at Winchester. For 30 years he was one of the most influential men in England and he became in rapid succession, a member of Henry Tudor's King's Council, Secretary of State, Lord Privy Seal and Bishop of Exeter, Durham and finally Winchester. He founded Corpus Christi College, Oxford with his own money and built and endowed grammar schools at Grantham and Taunton.

South Common, Lincoln

Introduction: A surprisingly varied walk considering its proximity to the city, across an open common, through a park, alongside a river and up the escarpment edge known locally as The Cliff, with a marvellous vista overlooking the Trent valley and possibly the finest view in the whole area of Lincoln cathedral set high upon the opposite hill.

Distance: 4½ miles of easy walking with one short, steep climb. OS Map Landranger Sheet 121 Lincoln.

Refreshments: The route passes The Plough Inn, Newark Road, Lincoln (Tel: Lincoln 520 340), which serves bar meals.

How to get there: Driving south of Lincoln across Pelham Bridge, turn right at the foot of Canwick Hill almost immediately after passing through the lights at the complicated road junction into South Park Road. Driving north into Lincoln on the B1131, turn left at the foot of Canwick Hill almost immediately after the T-junction traffic lights. Drive along South Park Road past the Youth Hostel as far as you can go to the very end of the cul-de-sac (GR 977 699).

The walk: Go through the iron handgate onto the common by the Golf Course sign and turn right to walk along the edge of the common aiming towards the spire of the redundant church currently being used as a DIY wholesale warehouse, keeping the abandoned railway line upon your immediate right at first.

Ignore the first footbridge by the school and proceed

towards the second bridge large enough to take vehicles. Cross the bridge and walk straight forward towards the toilet block and parking bay. Cross the busy main road and walk down Colegrave Street to turn right down Derby Street and then left along the footway to Laundry Bridge, leaving Sincil Drain and Bargate Sluice on your right.

Go over the bridge and turn left along the clear footpath with the river Witham on your left. After 700 yards turn right along a track leading into Boultham Park, keeping the small dyke on the left. At the bridge keep left and walk on until the large lake is on your right and then proceed straight forward with the recreation field and sand pit on your right. Go through the park entrance and turn immediately left down the tarmac track back to the river.

On reaching the river do not cross the bridge but turn right along the river bank all the way to the Plough Inn car park. Cross the main road once again to turn left over the bridge. Turn right at the end of the bridge along a good track with the river now on your right and unsuspected spoil-pit ponds on your left with lots of waterbirds.

After some 600 yards, by the battered sign warning people not to bathe at the outfall, turn left down the bank with yet another pond and recreation field on the left. Walk forward along the curved tarmac track until you reach Brant Road.

Cross Brant Road and turn left for about 100 yards and then right up the signposted bridleway, keeping the postbox on your left. At the field edge turn diagonally right across the old railway line and the field corner until you reach the hedge. Turn left uphill with the hedge on your right, through the iron handgate with a fierce spring (this is a bridleway) and continue up the steep slope to join the Viking Way path at the top.

Turn left at the top along the field edge with the fence and splendid house on your right, down into the dip to the first stile of the day. Cross the stile and continue along the top, to follow the path round to the right and, at the signposted broad track, keep straight on towards the road for 100 yards. Turn left along the clear track parallel to the road over the

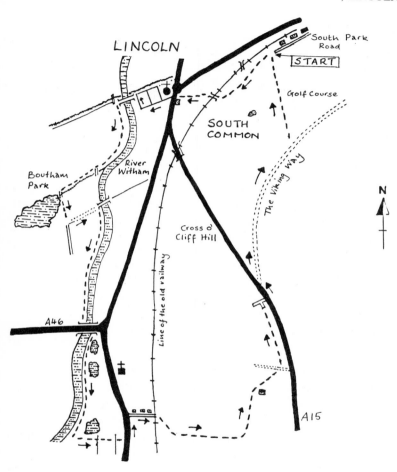

arable field aiming towards the white house.

In Coningsby Crescent turn right and on to Cross o' Cliff Road. Cross this busy road to turn left downhill for 100 yards. Turn right by the Lincoln City sign through the gate onto a clear path along the crest of the common. Walk along this attractive path for about 900 yards until you are level with the two ponds below and then turn left down the wooden and stone steps to walk diagonally right across the common, aiming towards the cathedral, until you reach your starting place. As you are coming back across the common the 11th century tower of St Peter at Gowts may be seen. Southey once wrote about the view of the cathedral from the top of the common: 'Never was an edifice more happily placed overtopping a city on the acclivity of a steep hill.'

Historical Notes

Eleanor Cross: At the foot of Cross o' Cliff Hill (where the toilet block now stands) once stood an Eleanor Cross 'without the city wall', close by the Gilbertine Priory of St Catherine's where the body of Queen Eleanor was embalmed by the nuns after being brought from Harby where she died in 1290. This was the first of the Eleanor Crosses to be erected at each halting place of the Queen's funeral procession, with Charing Cross in London (a corruption of the French Chere Reine, meaning 'Dear Queen') being the last. A four foot piece of the Lincoln cross was found on the common being used as a footbridge and it now resides at Lincoln Castle. Queen Eleanor's intestines were buried in a tomb in Lincoln Cathedral and her body in an identical tomb in Westminster Abbey.

The Roman Ermine Street came down the hill here to join the Roman Fosse Way where the common meets the road. This north west corner of the common is where the leper hospital of Holy Innocents stood, founded by Remigius and known as The Malandry. This great Roman road of the Fosse Way starts at Saltfleet on the coast, mentioned in Walk Twelve.

Bargate was one of the two gatehouses set in the medieval wall of the Sincil Dyke.

Boultham Park: In Roman times there were kilns at Boultham and the British Museum has examples of pottery found hereabouts. Today Boultham Park is 80 acres in extent.

Marton and the River Trent

Introduction: Marton lies where the straight 9 mile Roman road leading from Ermine Street comes to a ford built in the time of Hadrian over the river Trent, to the Roman station of Segelocum on the opposite bank. It is easy walking over the marsh along the Trent bank and on the cliff above the river. For a short walk it offers unexpected and panoramic views into Nottinghamshire and surprisingly varied country-side with a real sense of remoteness when walking over the wide sweep of marsh.

Distance: 3 miles but likely to be muddy in places after rain or a high tide. OS Map Landranger Sheet 121 Lincoln.

Refreshments: The Ingleby Arms, Marton (Torksey 246), which does not serve bar meals, but there is also the Hume Arms, Torksey (Torksey 613).

How to get there: Marton is situated on the A156 Gains-borough to Lincoln road, 6 miles from Gainsborough or 14 miles from Lincoln. Alternatively, from Scampton cross-roads along the straight 9-mile drive down the cliff via Tillbridge Lane and Stow Park Road through Sturton to Marton, then left at the crossroads to park off the main road by the church in Trent Port Road (GR 840 817).

The walk: From your parking place in the small layby by Marton church, walk away from the main road down Trent Port Lane with the church and the village playing fields on your left. Walk down to the river slipway and turn right along the track, just above the mean high water mark, that

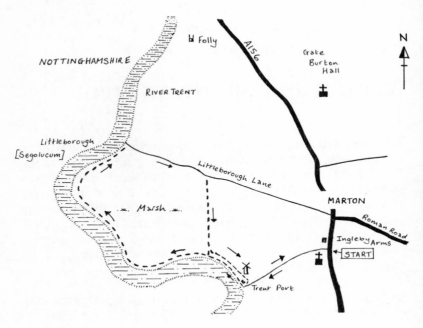

has recently been designated as a road used as a public path. Follow this track at the bottom of the cliff through the fieldgate and then turn right to the path junction and stile. (This track is the subject of a Map Modification Order. If it is obstructed take the signposted footpath by the windmill and turn left over the first stile.) Go over the stile on the left and onto the river embankment.

Follow the wide curve of the river for almost 1½ miles until you are directly opposite Littleborough on the Nottinghamshire bank of the river. After climbing the stile turn right down the very ancient green lane and Roman road known as Littleborough Lane for about 700 yards.

As the lane begins to ascend turn right on the signposted footpath to climb the stile and walk up the steep bank to the top of the cliff. Continue along the cliff edge that offers panoramic views; it is only some 10 or 15 metres above the flood plain but it appears much higher at this spot. After the second stile Marton church comes into view, then go over a third stile to continue along the cliff edge ignoring both the double fieldgate on the right and later the signpost and stile showing the way you have already walked. Walk on past the ruins of the old mill and on reaching Trent Port turn left to retrace your steps up the lane to the church and your starting place.

Historical Notes

St Margaret's church, Marton has a Saxon tower with fine herringbone masonry and a Norman arcade. The belfry windows are in typical Anglo-Saxon style. The tall cross in the churchyard now restored as a war memorial is said to have been an old market cross.

The river Trent: The Humber and the river Trent were one of the most important entry points for seasonal raiders from across the North Sea. Norsemen wintered at Torksey and constructed a temporary fort but gradually their policy changed from raids for plunder to permanent conquest. The riverside camp at Gainsborough became the headquarters for the conquest of England by King Swein of Denmark and his sons in 1013–1016.

A Roman milestone found in Bailgate, Lincoln recorded the distance of 14 miles to Segelocum (Littleborough). The Emperor Hadrian is reputed to have ordered the building of the river crossing and there was a Roman fort on the cliff to guard it.

King Harold of England and his house carls marched this way down the Roman road and across the river by the ford to fight William of Normandy in 1066, after they had defeated Harald Hardrada at the Battle of Stamford Bridge.

The Aegir or tidal bore may be seen on this stretch of river. It occurs at spring tides during the March and September equinox. It was so named by early Scandinavian settlers after their river god, Oegir. There was once a wharf, a corn warehouse, a malthouse and a working mill in the days of the flourishing river traffic at Trent Port but little remains today.

The 18th century Gate Burton Hall may be seen from the end of Littleborough Lane and, nearer to the river, the folly known as Burton Chateau.

The Civil War: Along the main road to Gainsborough Oliver Cromwell won a small but desperate victory on the 28th July 1643 that proved his reputation as a cavalry commander. In an attempt to relieve the Gainsborough garrison, besieged by Royalist forces, he defeated the young General Cavendish, a godson of Charles Stuart but then had to retreat when the Earl of Norwich approached the town with overwhelming forces. Cromwell fought a masterly rearguard action, halting and facing his pursuers on nine occasions along the road.

Nettleton On The Edge Of The Wolds

Introduction: This walk is an Area of Outstanding Natural Beauty with some wonderful views and an extraordinary sense of remoteness with invariably only rabbits and sheep for company. Nettleton lies under Mansgate Hill on the very edge of the Wolds with the busy Lincoln to Grimsby road running by the main village although not actually entering it. In the past the village supported nine water mills but there is little evidence of them today.

Rothwell, the only other village entered during the walk is actually the Cherry Valley Estate, where the hedges and fences are in perfect order and the whole area is a monument to its creator, the late Sir Joseph Nickerson.

Distance: This is a day walk of 9¾ or 10½ miles which should take about five hours with a break for refreshment, probably at Rothwell. OS Map Landranger Sheet 113 Grimsby.

Refreshments: Bar meals are available at both The Salutation Inn, Nettleton (Swallow 0472 371 300) and The Nickerson Arms, Rothwell (Caistor 0472 851 228), the latter open all day. There is a village store in both villages.

How to get there: Take the A46 Lincoln to Grimsby road and Nettleton village lies at the foot of Caistor Brow, 8 miles north of Market Rasen. The Salutation Inn, Nettleton, on the A46 at the foot of the hill leading up to Caistor, is the start of the walk and the landlord has kindly agreed that walkers may leave their cars on the car park providing they use the section furthest away from the entrance to the inn. But it is always a good idea to check with the landlord before you leave your car in the pub car park and go for a walk (GR 106 002).

The walk: From the car park walk down to the road junction and turn left along Church Street into the village, with the post office and village store on your right and the ancient weatherworn church on the left. Continue along the village street to bear right round the bend after 200 yards and forward for a ¼ mile to a fork in the road just beyond Whitestone Cottage. Turn left up Grange Farm track with the horned helmet of the Viking Way route mark showing the way. Go through the gates beyond Grange Farm to follow the track uphill with old farm buildings on your right. The Viking Way turns right alongside the lake and follows the beck up the valley; this is your return route. Your way forward leads uphill for almost a mile until you reach the old highway known as Caistor High Street.

Cross the road and go through the bridleway gate to continue forward along the field edge with the hedge on your immediate left. Go directly across the next road and through the wide gap in the hedge opposite Rothwell Grange Farm sign. Proceed diagonally right across the arable field at first parallel to the hedge on the left and continue straight forward on this line aiming for the end of the hedge on the right by the track. At this track junction take the good track forward in the same direction with the hedge upon your right. At the cross hedge keep straight on along the raised headland towards the Badger Hills for another 600 yards. Pelham Pillar may be seen over on the left and the Humber Bank industrial plants straight ahead.

At the track junction turn right on the bridleway towards Rothwell Stackgarth abandoned farmhouse and buildings and go straight over the cross track downhill on the good farm track with the hedge on your left. Turn left at the road into the village and the Hickerson Arms.

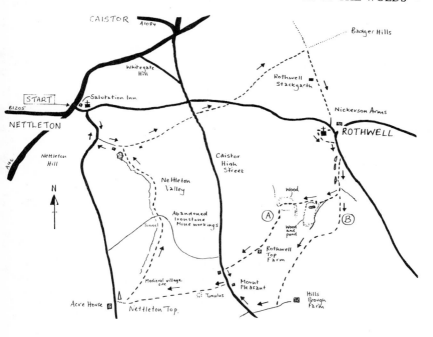

Cross the road out of the Nickerson Arms car park up the cul-de-sac of School Lane where the old village school has now become the village hall. At the top of the lane turn left into the most attractive churchyard and, after inspecting the church and some of the gravestones, follow the gravelled path down to the road.

Turn right at the road for 150 yards and then right on the signposted bridleway with a bridleway gate alongside the locked fieldgate, for it is a private road but a public path. Follow this pleasant metalled track up the valley with the series of ponds and nature reserve area on the right. After about 1,000 yards you have the choice of continuing uphill on this attractive track or following the slightly longer but much wilder and even more attractive bridlepath up the valley on the left.

For the *shorter metalled route (A)* continue uphill with an estate-made footpath sign (on a bridleway) directing you to keep to the metalled track around the wood edge. At the copse containing the odd concrete plaque on the left indicating 'Great Walk 1951–1974', turn sharp left up the valley to Rothwell Top Farm. Turn right by the farm buildings and continue on the same metalled track with the hedge on the right until you meet Caistor High Street once more. Turn left down the road for 250 yards until you reach the white house known as Mount Pleasant.

For the *longer alternative route (B)* turn left off the metalled track with the hedge on your immediate left and walking parallel to the woodland over on the right. The junction is waymarked. At the end of the hedge on the left walk straight forward to turn right up the valley on the right along a clear track clinging to the valley side with a wooden fence above you on the left. After about 700 yards from your turning point go through the gap in the hedge by the waymark to follow the clearly defined grass track up to the narrowing head of the valley to the metalled farm lane with a small covert on the left. Turn right to Caistor High Street and then right along the road for 700 yards to the white painted house known as Mount Pleasant.

Cross the road and go through the bridleway gate with the hedge on the left and after a mile see way across the field on the left the utterly alien radar scanner intruding into the countryside. Follow this bridleway until you go through the metal gate at the head of the valley on the right. Turn right through the hills and hollows of the medieval village site to join the Viking Way footpath with Nettleton Beck on the left as you descend. Go over a number of stiles and through the tunnel with the road leading to the old mine above, through the wild patch of scrubland to turn left on the track for a few yards and then right again to continue downhill with the lake at the bottom just before Grange Farm. Turn left on the track leading to Grange Farm and right at the road into Nettleton village and back to your starting place, with an opportunity for well earned refreshment if you have timed it right.

Historical Notes

Pelham Pillar seen from the walk is 128 ft high and com-memorates the astonishing feat of Charles Anderson Pelham, first Lord Yarborough, who planted no fewer than 12,552,700 trees on his Lincolnshire estates.

Rothwell is an 'estate village' dominated by Cherry Valley Farms, created by the late Sir Joseph Nickerson who rose from being a coalman in Caistor to command a very success-ful international enterprise and became nationally renowned in fieldsports. His unusual grave is in Rothwell churchyard.

Nettleton: At the top of Nettleton Valley there are hollows and humps in the field above the spring, all that is left of the medieval village of Wykeham – perhaps abandoned because of the Black Death or emptied by a search for easier ground.

Chalk on top of sand provides an unstable combination, which has settled or shifted over the years to form long terraces running high above the valley. Towards the end of the 17th century 25 of Nettleton's houses were smothered by sand creeping down the hillside.

In those days all Nettleton's land was contained in two 1,000 acre fields that stretched from the village for 2 miles up the valley sides to the source of the beck. When the land was enclosed in the 1790s the villagers found their common land was hedged about and cultivated and their rents increased dramatically to pay for the cost of the enclosure.

The last ironstone was extracted in 1969 and grass and trees have reclaimed some of the old mine workings.

The weatherbeaten tower of Nettleton's church was built at the end of the Saxon period and the top stage and buttresses were added in the 15th century.

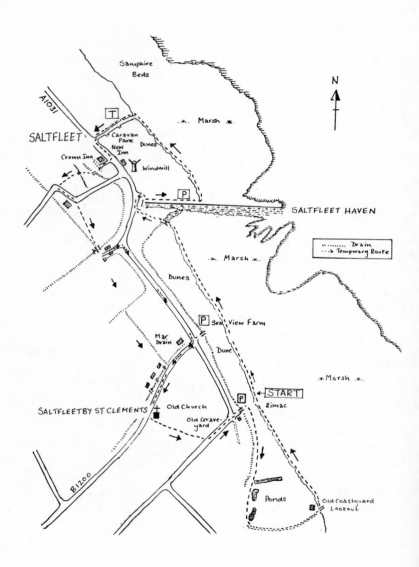

N

Samphire Beds

A1031

SALTFLEET

Crown Inn

Caravan Park
New Inn

T

Windmill

Dunes

.*. Marsh .*.

P

SALTFLEET HAVEN

.... Drain
---> Temporary Route

.*. Marsh .*.

Dunes

P Sea View Farm

Mar Drain

Dune

.*. Marsh .*.

SALTFLEETBY ST CLEMENTS ✝ Old Church

P START

Old Grave-
yard

Rimac

B1200

Ponds

Old Coastguard
Lookout

Saltfleet

Introduction: An exhilarating walk along the coast, from Rimac to the ancient town of Saltfleet. This is a walk for nature lovers, for part of it is on a National Nature Reserve where you are permitted free access. There are extensive views over the shore and reclaimed marshland. During the month of June there is usually a wonderful display of marsh orchids, and at all times of the year an array of wild flowers.

Distance: 7 miles taking about 3½ hours with time to 'stand and stare' and some refreshment en route. OS Map Landranger Sheet 113 Grimsby.

Refreshments: The New Inn, Main Road, Saltfleet (0507 338603) and the Crown Inn, Pump Lane, Saltfleet (0507 338412) serve bar meals. There is a restaurant at the redundant church at Saltfleetby St Clements but only during the main holiday season.

How to get there: Rimac Car Park and Nature Reserve is across the bridge over the river Eau at the sharp right-angled bend on the A1031 road 1½ miles south of Saltfleet. This is on the winding coast road (A1031) from Mablethorpe to Cleethorpes some 7 miles north of Mablethorpe or 11 miles east of Louth on the B1200 (GR 468 917).

The walk: From Rimac car park go through the kissing gate and then over the stile on the right. Keep along the foot of the dunes and through another kissing gate. Wind round in the hollows until you sight the abandoned Coastguard Station and follow any path towards it, with an old concrete machine gun post on the right and the ponds that are the home of the natterjack toad on the left. This is the most proflic area for marsh orchids. Turn left at the sandy track to the ruin of the former Coastguard Station.

Walk down the concrete slipway and turn left along the shore line by the Ministry of Defence warning notice regarding the Air to Ground range. Ignore the track on the left to Sea View Farm and continue along the shore-line to the large concrete bridge at the Great Eau outfall and Paradise. There is a sign here at the Black Gowt Sluice – 'Paradise: No caravans or camping'. On reaching Saltfleet Haven turn right at the road to cross the bridge and right again to walk towards the sea with the Great Eau now on your immediate right.

After ½ mile of walking towards the sea and some 125 yards beyond the car park and picnic site turn left off the road on the seaward side of the foot of the sandhills for ¾ mile and then left up the concrete ramp to Sea Lane with a large caravan park on the left. Toilets, a beach shop and a cafe are down this lane. Walk down Sea Lane to turn left at the Main Road towards Saltfleet and the Crown Inn, with the New Inn a little further along the road by the refurbished windmill. The village pump in the square is dedicated to a local man who was severely wounded at Clenso in the South African war.

From the Crown Hotel turn right down Pump Lane to the wooden footbridge on the right at the very end of the lane. Walk across the field on a defined path to the bushes and on to the concrete bridge at the bend in the road. Turn left on the road towards the farm and then right off the road at the bend over the wooden footbridge with the farmhouse and drain now on your right. Walk along the drain edge until you reach the old brick bridge with the white dome of the windmill away on your left.

After crossing the brick bridge and the connecting track walk straight forward with the drain on your left ONLY IF IT IS SIGNPOSTED, for, at the end of the next field, a bridge over the Mar Dyke is required. The bridge has been promised but had not been built at the time of writing. If it is NOT signposted, turn left down the track and then right at the road for ¾ mile before turning right at the road junction towards Saltfleetby St Clement's church. If the bridge is built, follow the edge of the dyke, cross the bridge and proceed to the road to turn right to the church.

The redundant church of Saltfleetby St Clement's is now a restaurant, open during the main holiday season. Turn left through the lychgate, through the churchyard and straight forward with a small dyke on your right. There is a curious abandoned and overgrown churchyard in the copse of trees on the left. Walk diagonally across the field to the fieldgate and turn left on the road back to Rimac and your starting place.

Historical Notes

Glasswort, the 'samfer' of Lincolnshire and other east coast marshes, is found along this shore for the mile-wide Skidbrooke foreshore provides ideal conditions for growth. Centuries ago samphire was burnt to provide ash which was an impure carbonate of soda for mixing with sand in the glass making process. Today it is eaten as an asparagus-like starter to a meal, or for a real traditional Lincolnshire dish it needs to be pickled and eaten with stuffed chine or boiled bacon.

Saltfleet was the principal port in the Roman province Flavia Caesarienses. From here commenced the Fosse Way, the great Roman road leading from the North Sea to Exeter, via Lincoln and Newark. 'Salt' is Icelandic, 'fleet' from the Saxon 'a place where the tide comes in'. In the reign of Edward III, in 1359, the Royal Port of Saltfleet furnished two ships and 49 men for the invasion of Brittany.

Saltfleet was a busy market town in days gone by. Part of the old town and its church are said to have been washed away by the sea and the lonely church at Skidbrooke was used for worship. Stones that were once part of the church are sometimes washed up on the shore and, on one occasion, the big clapper of a church bell was caught in a fisherman's net. There is an astonishing stretch of sand at low tide, when the sea may be hardly visible from the land.

Saltfleetby St Clements, the smallest of the Saltfleets and the nearest to the sea, has a small church built partly from the ruin of a 700 year old house of prayer. The church is now redundant and has been converted into a small restaurant that is only open during the summer season.

Rimac Nature Reserve is the only Lincolnshire home of the natterjack toad. In June there is a wonderful display of marsh orchids near to the Rimac car park, in autumn the bright orange berries of the sea buckthorn can be seen and many other salt loving wild flowers may be viewed at other times of the year.

Snipedales Country Park and Tennyson Country

Introduction: The 120-acre Snipedales Nature Reserve is managed by the Lincolnshire and South Humberside Trust for Nature Conservation and the adjoining Country Park offers picturesque walks through 90 acres of woodland consisting mainly of Corsican pine with a few Scots pine. Many broad-leaved trees and shrubs have recently been planted to give more diversity. The wide ride which runs to the north east corner of the park has some magnificent ash trees. Snipedales is situated on the southern edge of the Wolds and consists of steep sided valleys fretted by streams which have cut through the soft Spilsby sandstone down to the Kimmeridge clay below. At the junction of the sandstone and the clay are spring lines giving rise to small streams. This lovely walk takes one through the Country Park and a section of the Nature Reserve, then across open fields and green lanes to Hagworthingham and Bag Enderby, with its Tennyson connections.

Distance: 8 miles with a shorter alternative of 5 miles, mainly easy walking on green lanes and good paths with only one short, steep section. OS Map Landranger Sheet 122 Skegness.

Refreshments: There is a roadside cafe in Hagworthingham Main Street, and the George and Dragon public house, Hagworthingham (Tel: Winceby 0507 588255) serves bar meals. Nowhere else en route.

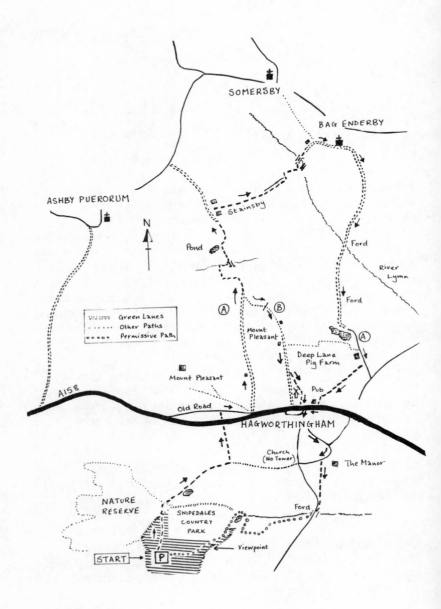

SOMERSBY

BAG ENDERBY

ASHBY PUERORUM

Stainsby

N

Pond

Ford

River
Lymn

Ford

Green Lanes
Other Paths
Permissive Path

Ⓐ Ⓑ

Mount
Pleasant

Deep Lane
Pig Farm

Ⓐ

Mount Pleasant

A158

Old Road

Pub

HAGWORTHINGHAM

Church
(No Tower)

The Manor

NATURE
RESERVE

SNIPEDALES
COUNTRY
PARK

Ford

Viewpoint

START → P

How to get there: Take the A158 Horncastle to Skegness road to turn off onto the A1115 Spilsby road at the top of Winceby Hill and follow this road for 2 miles with Snipedales Country Park up a track on the left if proceeding towards Spilsby. Do not stop at the first small car park for Snipedales Nature Reserve opposite the telephone kiosk. The Country Park car park has toilets, a picnic site and display boards. (GR 330 682.)

The walk: From the car park follow the narrow path behind the toilet block, turning left to a footbridge and uphill on the Red Route. Climb the steps and continue to follow the red waymarks. Turn into the Nature Reserve, down the steps and right on the path downhill over wired decking across low-lying ground to the Waterside Vegetation information board. Thirty yards beyond the notice board turn left up a steep bank and at the top turn right on the signposted public footpath down to a bridge and stile.

After crossing the bridge climb straight forward up the valley side and at the top go across to the isolated stile standing in the field (there used to be a field edge here) and then across to another stile visible in the remaining hedge. Go down into the dip and up the other slope to bear slightly right at the top and then straight forward on a clear path. When you meet the hedge turn left down the track junction with the hedge now on your left, to a stile and signpost on the main road.

Cross the road and go through the gap in the hedge opposite onto the old road. Turn right towards Hagworthingham. At the road turn left uphill on the lane to Mount Pleasant, with a tiny old bungalow with a wonderful view on the left at the top of the hill. A little further on ignore the track on the left but pause to look at the wide panorama across the Wolds.

For the shorter route (B) turn right off the track on a signposted path with the hedge on your right, to walk down the field to a stile and signpost in the dip. Go over the stile and diagonally right on the defined path towards Partridge

Cottage (not the farm over on the left), that is at first concealed by a rise in the ground. The path brings you onto the lane just to the left of the cottage. Turn right up this hollow way and then left off the lane on a signposted footpath leading to the mill. Follow this overgrown footpath for a few yards down to the main road. Cross the road by the little green to rejoin the longer route on the corner of Church Lane (see below).

For the longer route (A) walk down the hillside to turn left round the field edge, down to the stream and right along the stream bank until you come to a footbridge. This odd U-shaped route is a diversion, for the path at one time went straight across the field to the bridge. Cross the bridge and walk straight forward with the hedge on the right to turn right at the track junction on a waymarked route with the pond on the left. Follow this good farm track all the way to Stainsby House, ignoring the stoned track on the right.

At Stainsby turn right off the track on the signposted path between the farm buildings. Follow this farm track down and when it turns to the right leave the track to turn left on the footpath with the hedge on your immediate left. At the end of this field (waymark) continue to the left with the hedge still on the left and then down along a dog-leg to the stream and a narrow concrete bridge. If this is too over-grown there is a stout sleeper-constructed bridge a few yards away. Walk up the good green lane towards Bag Enderby church on the right.

If you wish, there is a public footpath by the side of the end cottage on the left that leads you to Somersby where ten Tennyson children were born. Dr Tennyson came here in 1808 as rector for Somersby and Bag Enderby. You can return to Bag Enderby by the lane.

From Bag Enderby church turn left from the church porch and go straight forward on a signposted path with the farm on the right. Follow this green lane round the bend to the right and down to the ford over the infant river Lymn – the brook of Tennyson's poem 'The Brook'.

Continue up the green lane ignoring the track to the left.

Pass the second ford over a tributary stream and the lake on the right and go up the slope as quickly as possible past the pig farm! Turn right off the lane some 500 yards beyond the farm on a signposted path and aim to the left by a telegraph post in the field corner and an inadequate stile. Walk towards the house and follow the track down to the road with The George and Dragon on the right, with the cafe a little further along the main road.

Cross the busy road and turn right for 350 yards and then left down Church Lane. *The shorter route joins here.* Walk down Church Lane for 150 yards and then turn left up Bond Hayes Lane and right at the lane junction for another 150 yards.

Where the road bends to the right, turn left along the track leading to The Manor with a house at the side named Hacberd. Just beyond the house garden on the right climb the stile and follow the path down to another stile. The pond on the left is due for rehabilitation. Walk down the slope to the splendid new bridge to turn right to the lane and the ford. This is a good apple stop.

Cross the road and follow the new permissive path along-side the stream on your right. Follow this clear track with new fencing round in a U-shape just before the wood. Apparently this odd route around three sides of a field was deliberately done to provide walkers with a view from the higher ground. At the bottom of the slope enter the Country Park once more by the new wooden gate and stile. Follow this narrow path through the trees on the red waymarked route up the valley with the stream on the left. Turn left briefly at the ponds and follow the track uphill with the stream and ponds now on your right. There is one side path that leads you to a viewpoint where you can see Mount Pleasant and the way you have walked. Retrace your steps down the steep slope back to your original path to turn left down and up the steps to the car park and your starting place.

Historical Notes

Lord Tennyson: An unconventional upbringing and the countryside of his childhood, where you can walk, had a marked effect upon Alfred Lord Tennyson, the Victorian Poet Laureate. He was born in the rectory at Somersby in 1809 which was the family home for the next 29 years. Alfred's father was an embittered man in that his father had disinherited him in favour of his younger brother and, against his will, forced him to become a cleric. By the time Alfred was eleven the family had grown to eleven children and they often had to sleep 'five or six to a room'. Somersby House as it is now named can be seen from the Bag Enderby green lane and the rambling old house has changed little although: 'The seven elms, the poplars four, That stand beside my father's door' in his *Ode to Memory* are no longer there.

From the age of six Alfred Tennyson went to Louth Grammar School which he apparently hated, refusing in later years to walk down the lane past it. His education after leaving Louth was conducted entirely at home by Dr Tennyson, his father, until he went to Cambridge. *In Memoriam* tells of his sorrow at departing from Somersby:

'We leave the well-beloved place
Where first we gazed upon the sky
The roofs that heard our earliest cry
Will shelter one of stranger race.'

At **Bag Enderby** the iron boss of a Danish shield discovered in a nearby field may be seen fixed to the ancient door. The font in the church is worth examining for its quaint carving and there are often Tennyson memorabilia on display.

Hagworthingham deserves better than to be called Hag. The name means hill fortress at the commencement of the 'hag' – broken ground in a moss or bog. The windmill seen from the walk and visited on the shorter route is now capped and is a reminder of the milling and merchant business of a local family called Ellis. The parish church tower collapsed in 1972 and the peal of eight bells were sold in order to raise money for the repair of the tower. Above the Hagworthingham ford on the lane leading to Lusby is the site of an ancient burial mound. The Old Hall on the Main Road is an 18th century house and the New Hall is also Georgian.

Stockwith Mill, no longer used for its original purpose, is mentioned by Tennyson in his poem *The Brook*. The buildings, which are 18th century, are used as a restaurant and craft shop and there are three waymarked short walks.

Winceby lies at the head of the valley containing Snipedales Nature Reserve and on the 11th October 1643 Oliver Cromwell fought and won a major cavalry action here against the Royalist forces. As a result Bolingbroke Castle surrendered, the siege of Hull was lifted and practically all of Lincolnshire went over to the side of Parliament. The lane is still known as Slash Lane from the pursuit of fleeing Royalists by Parliamentary troopers.

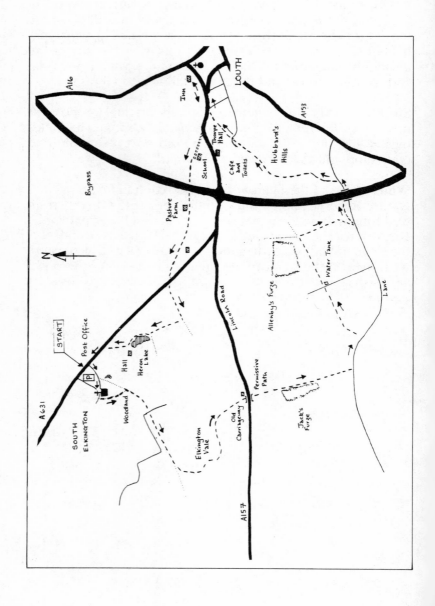

South Elkington and Louth

Introduction: This walk begins in the small village of South Elkington, situated in some of the most attractive country-side in Eastern England and designated an Area of Outstanding Natural Beauty. Here the seasons provide an ever-changing tapestry with chalk showing through the green and brown slopes so characteristic of this part of Lincolnshire in the early part of the year, later the harsh golden colour of oil-seed rape, then fields of waving corn in summer followed by the many different tints of the wood in autumn. The route takes you down the valley and towards the major objective of the walk – the attractive market town of Louth with its far-famed church steeple, a landmark for miles around.

Distance: 8½ miles of mainly good walking with some cross-field public footpaths. It is likely to be muddy in the wood-land at times, so stout shoes or boots are desirable. OS Map Landranger Sheet 122 Skegness.

Refreshments: There is a village store and post office in South Elkington, and the complete range of shops and inns in Louth, with toilets and a cafe (in season) at the exit to Hubbard's Hills.

How to get there: South Elkington is on the A631 Louth to Market Rasen road some 2½ miles west of Louth. Car parking has been arranged for individuals (not groups) in the grounds of South Elkington village store by courtesy of the shopkeeper. But it would be a politeness to the shop to check on the day that this is still permissible. Bed and breakfast is also available. (GR 297 885.)

The walk: Turn right out of the post office grounds away from the main road into the village and continue forward to the church past the ornate village institute hall. Have a look in the church and churchyard and then leave by the rear exit. On the left you will find a signposted footpath and stile leading you down to the wood. Enter the wood and turn right immediately to follow the waymarked track up the short, steep hill and then, on leaving the wood turn left to follow the field edge.

On meeting the broad track with signposts, cross to proceed straight forward on the clear bridlepath through the wood edge with the stream and the broad farm track on the right. Avoid tracks to the left and right until you eventually turn down the valley on almost reaching the wood edge. There are ponds on your right after a short way and you are now walking down Elkington Vale which was the old carriageway to the hall. Near the road turn right from the house to a stile and signpost with the road bridge on your right. Cross the Lincoln road and over the stile on the waymarked permissive path by courtesy of the Hallington Farming Co.

At the top of the hil by Jack's Furze after about an hour's walking you get your first glimpse of St James's spire in Louth. Do not omit to look back over the lovely undulating country behind you. This is a good apple stop.

At the road turn left downhill towards Louth (there is a triangulation pillar nearby at the time of writing, at 364 ft) and after 350 yards turn left off the road on a signposted footpath just before the bend in the road. On this cross-field path aim towards the church spire and a four-barred gate with stile with a brick water tank on the right. Walk straight forward with the hedge on your left parallel to Allenby's Furze. Turn right on meeting the bridlepath with a hedge now on your right. At the fieldgate the exact route of the path is to the right as far as the bridleway gate to the road and then left on the footpath with the hedge on your right into the field corner on the right by the bypass bridge.

Turn left under the bypass and, after only a few yards, left again through the wooden gate into Hubbard's Hills to either walk along the top of the slope on the right or by the stream at the bottom of the steep valley, for both are equally attractive. Keep along the tarmac track in the valley bottom until the end of the park where there are toilets and, in season, a cafe. Turn right over the bridge onto the path with the stream on your right. Fifty yards beyond the white house on the left, near where the hill path joins, turn left off the road through the wicket gate and follow the tarmac track through the open parkland.

At the road turn right as far as the junction and then left up Westgate with Breakneck Lane on the right proceeding towards St James's church and the ancient Wheatsheaf Inn that does bar food and is well worth a visit. Have a look at the church and the blue plaque on the rectory opposite. The distance given is as far as the church but you may wish to explore the town further.

Turn right out of The Wheatsheaf to walk back the way you came but bear right along the main road over the bridge spanning the river Lud, round the bend and up the hill to the left still on the main road. Turn right up the driveway to Deighton Close School on the signposted footpath and to the left of the farm buildings belonging to Thorpe Hall. There is a huge waymark here, then some newly built step stiles leading onto the bypass. Cross the road and the stile on the opposite side and walk forward past Pasture Farm house on the right and yet another step stile.

Continue straight forward at the beginning of Cow Pasture Wood and take a last look at Louth parish church spire. Climb the stile and enter the wood to drop down across the open field to a white handgate and the Market Rasen road.

Cross the road and walk straight forward down the valley to double fieldgates and a footbridge at the side without any stiles at each end. After crossing the bridge bear diagonally right up the valley with the stream and then the fence on your right. At the white handgate and stile turn right on a good track with Heron Lake on your left. Walk to the road on the right. Cross and turn left along the footway to the war memorial and your starting place.

Historical Notes

South Elkington: Heron Lake is an attractive spot frequented in season by many fishermen. Have a look at South Elkington war memorial and check the date of the end of World War One.

According to the will of Margaret Sheffelde who died in 1531 in South Elkington, the church of All Saints was known in the past as 'All Halloys'. Only the church tower dates from the medieval period but today it remains a lovely peaceful place. In the well-kept graveyard near the lychgate grows an unusual thorny tree, the honey locust, planted to remind us of Christ's crown of thorns and known as the Calvary Tree for it came from Palestine. It is on the site of a former Anglo-Saxon burial ground which is not unusual with All Saints churches. The Angles settled here in the 6th and 7th centuries before their conversion to Christianity and nearly a hundred pagan burial urns have been unearthed in the area.

Elkington Vale is the old carriageway to the hall and follows the steeply wooded valley to the road leading to Lincoln. Along the carriageway are several magnificent coast redwoods, trees native to the Pacific Coast of North America but surviving in the comparatively dry Lincolnshire climate.

The river Lud: To the west of Louth the river Lud winds through the wooded gorge known as Hubbard's Hills, a natural park of some 40 acres given to the town by Auguste Alphonse Pahud. A beech clad precipice on one side with the path on top, faces meadows sloping up to the woods.

Lude, modern Louth, meant 'the loud one' referring to the noise of the river when in flood. In 1920 a cloudburst on the Wolds caused water to rush down the valley in overwhelming torrents carrying away bridges and wrecking many houses. Many people were drowned for the river rose 15 ft in a remarkably short time and it sank almost as rapidly as it had risen.

Louth, 'this jewel of a town' derives its name from the river Lud, the 'd' of which is pronounced in Scandinavian as 'th'. Ethelred, the first Archbishop of Canterbury originated from Louth for he was the abbot of an 8th century monastery in the town.

At a magnificent 295 ft the spire of St James's church, Louth is claimed to be the highest parish church spire in the land. Built around 1501–1515 this beautiful spire dominates the town and the surrounding countryside and may be seen from the walk. The original weathercock on the spire was fixed in 1515 amid great rejoicing for it was made from a copper basin which was part of the booty captured at Flodden Field from James IV of Scotland. John Betjeman wrote: 'The magnificent church is one of the last great medieval masterpieces.'

The people of Louth took part in the Lincolnshire Rising of 1536 against the dissolution of the monasteries by Henry VIII, when a letter from the king described the men of Lincolnshire as 'rude commons of one of the most brute and beastly shires of the whole realm.' Several of the townsmen were put to death at Louth and Thomas Kendall the vicar was hanged at Tyburn.

The Greenwich Meridian passes through Lincolnshire and there are two places at least where it is marked. One is on the sea wall between Cleethorpes and Humberstone and the other is marked by a plaque on the wall of a shop in Eastgate, Louth, plus a metal strip on the pavement. The word 'meridian' derives from the Latin 'meridies' – midday and the prime or first meridian is used as a line from which world time is measured.

Elizabethan **Thorpe Hall**, nestling among fine trees above the old town on the Lincoln road near the entrance to Deighton Close School, was built by Sir John Bolle in 1584. He was the hero of the ballad of 'The Spanish Lady of High Degree', of whom he had charge after the siege of Cadiz. She fell in love with her captor and because of her unrequited love for the English knight, who was already married, she retired to a nunnery, although it is said that she haunts the hall and grounds as 'The Green Lady', having followed him back to England.

Tattershall Castle and Tattershall Thorpe

Introduction: Tattershall is a busy village situated between the rivers Witham and Bain and dominated by the imposing brick keep of Tattershall Castle, a landmark for many miles over the surrounding fen. This walk is a pleasant riverside stroll on the very edge of the Fen, across an abandoned railway line, through two important ancient woodland sites and along a newly created public footpath linking Tattershall Carr Wood and Tattershall Thorp Carr Wood, belonging to The Woodland Trust. There are many reminders of the part played by Lincolnshire as 'bomber county' in the Second World War.

Distance: 5 miles of easy walking, say three hours, with a stop for refreshment and an opportunity to visit Holy Trinity church. The walk could be reduced by 1¾ miles by not going to the second wood and Tattershall Thorpe but it would be a pity to do so. OS Map Landranger Sheet 122 Skegness.

Refreshments: Available at the Lodge Cafe and public houses in, or near, the Market Place, Tattershall, and The Bluebell Inn (Coningsby 342 206) at Tattershall Thorpe (bar food).

How to get there: Tattershall Market Place is 14 miles from Sleaford on the A153 Horncastle road or 10 miles south of Horncastle on the A153 Sleaford road, with the possibility of using secondary roads, via Woodhall Spa. (GR 213 579.)

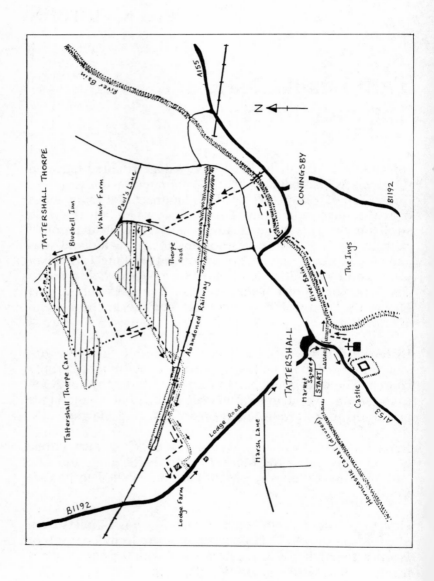

The walk: From the Market Place walk past the telephone kiosk and the 15th century market cross to turn right along the Sleaford Road towards the collegiate church and castle. Just before the castle entrance turn left on the gravelled, fenced track leading to the church alongside the castle drive with the Bede Houses (1440) on the left.

From the church entrance follow the paved path behind the Bede Houses with the bowling green on your right. Turn right to the river with the choked canal on your left and after crossing the metal bridge above the weir turn left along the good embankment path for about ¾ mile until you reach the main road. Cross the road and Coningsby Bridge to follow the signposted path through the metal kissing gate on the other bank of the river with the river Bain now on your right. Over the stile at the next bridge, turn left up the metalled track known as Mason's Lane. Look back here at the famous one-fingered clock on Coningsby church tower.

Walk straight across the road and over the step stile on the signposted path with the hedge on your immediate left. Climb the next stile and up the embankment of the disused railway and down the steps on the far side and across the field to Thorpe Road. Turn right at the lane towards Tattershall Thorpe.

At the bend in the road a few yards before the road junction with Paul's Lane turn left into Tattershall Carr Wood. The Woodland Trust notice states: 'Visitors are welcome to walk in the wood.' After 200 yards turn right a few yards beyond the abandoned war-time bunker to follow a clear track by the right-hand edge of the wood. After another 200 yards, avoiding any tracks to the left, continue around the wood edge past a second ammunition bay and four air raid shelters and on to the track junction by the edge of the wood.

For the shorter version of the walk continue forward here. Otherwise look out for the path on the right to lead you out of the wood, cross the stout footbridge and into the open field with Woodland Trust trees planted on each side of the track. Half way across this field at the track crossroads turn right on the good farm track which is a public right of way and walk towards the white painted building on the left which is the ancient Bluebell Inn.

Turn left out of the inn along Thorpe Road for 250 yards and left again into the wood by the commemorative mill-stone and almost immediately right in front of the derelict RAF buildings along a concrete track. Turn left at the end and Thorpe Camp Preservation Group's wire mesh perimeter fence is on the right. Walk straight forward over another ditchboard with a Woodland Trust welcome sign-board. After 30 yards turn right to cross a ditchboard and left again on a tarmac track for about 300 yards, then turn left across the wood with an old bunker on the right just before you leave the wood. Continue straight across the open field on a good track made by the Woodland Trust to link the two woods.

After crossing the stout wooden footbridge once again and re-entering Tattershall Carr Wood (*joining the shorter route here*), turn right on a clear path at first along the wood edge and finally between two ponds. Leave the wood to turn right on the former railway trackbed for a few yards and follow the farm track around to the left to proceed with the abandoned railway cutting now on your right. The public right of way actually crosses this cutting but the drainage has gone and it is invariably flooded. The path then crosses the arable field and goes behind Lodge Farm buildings where it is overgrown and ill-defined. Therefore, at this stage, it is wiser to keep to the permissive farm track all the way to Lodge Road by following it round to the left with the hedge on your right and past the farm buildings. Turn left on reaching the lane and back to the Market Square.

Historical Notes

Tattershall: In 1201 a charter was granted for the holding of a weekly market at Tattershall by King John in return for a trained goshawk. The first castle was begun about 1230 by Robert of Tateshale, a descendant of Eudo, the Norman lord of the manor. The impressive castle, of which only the keep and the guardroom remain today, was built in 1440 by the Lord Treasurer, Ralph Cromwell. He had fought alongside Henry V at Agincourt and returned home from the wars in France to hold high office. He became Chamberlain of the Exchequer, Master of the King's Falcons, Constable of Nottingham Castle, Warden of Sherwood Forest and Lord High Treasurer of England, and for a great number of years he was the power behind the throne.

While he was Lord Treasurer to Henry VI he transformed the old castle at Tattershall into a home for himself, founded the college and supervised the building of the church and restoration of the almshouses. The college was built primarily to house the people employed to pray for the souls of Lord Cromwell's family and friends. All that remains of the collegiate buildings are the fragments of brickwork adjoining the chancel but the almshouses which were founded before Lord Cromwell's time remain, for they were re-endowed by him and rebuilt in 1485. They are now occupied by six people.

Holy Trinity church is a vast place close by the castle and the 550th anniversary of the building was celebrated in 1989. There are more than 60 windows through which the light streams unhindered for most of the stained glass was removed to Stamford in the 18th century. There is a burial slab in the nave to Tom Thumb.

Tattershall Picnic Place (with toilets) is ½ mile along the road from the castle and it was once a section of the Boston to Lincoln railway. The railway superseded the steam packet along the river Witham that took passengers and goods between the two places in about six hours. The railway only took 1 hour and 29 minutes and, as a result, the steam packet trade diminished and eventually ceased in 1860. It is an attractive area with flooded 'borrow' pits where soil was excavated to build the railway embankments, wandering paths and wide open spaces.

The Bluebell Inn is an ancient hostelry on a drovers road and possesses a priest-hole relic of the Civil War. The hostelry has RAF connections from nearby Coningsby airfield that was home to Mosquito Pathfinder Squadrons and the Dambusters in the Second World War. Guy Gibson was killed flying one of their aircraft in September, 1944.

The Horncastle Canal was opened in September 1802 ten years after work had started. The canal was used for carrying agricultural products including grain and malt from Horncastle to the Witham and on to Lincoln or the port of Boston. Later the canal was used to carry materials to build the Great Northern Railway branch line from Kirkstead to Horncastle. Today the canal is a valuable wild life habitat.

The Green Lanes of Temple Bruer

Introduction: This fascinating walk begins at the lonely church of Temple Bruer, situated at the junction of five lanes, some of them unsurfaced green lanes that provide fine walking across the Heath in all weathers. The route then crosses Ermine Street Roman road, built by the Ninth Legion in AD 50 and known hereabouts as the High Dyke, that has now become part of the Viking Way long distance recreational path. As the area is underlain by Lincolnshire limestone, which is a porous rock, there are few streams on the surface of the sandy soil, which contains many fragments of limestone. Limestone is still quarried in the area and many houses and field boundaries locally are built in this stone. The walk returns past the preceptory of the Knights Templars, who founded the village in the 12th century.

Distance: 7½ miles omitting the preceptory or 9¼ miles via the preceptory, Temple Farm and Warren Houses, mainly on good tracks but with two sections of defined cross-field paths. OS Map Landranger Sheet 121 Lincoln.

Refreshments: The Marquis of Granby Inn, Wellingore (Tel: Lincoln 0522 810442) is nearest for bar meals. There is a range of shops and other public houses further in the village but nowhere else en route.

How to get there: Taking the A15 Sleaford to Lincoln road, Temple Bruer is signposted 6½ miles from Sleaford or 10 miles from Lincoln. Alternatively, take the A607 Lincoln to

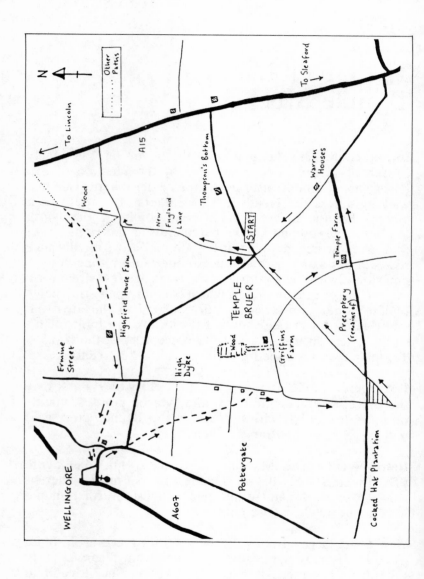

Grantham road as far as Wellingore village and then follow by-roads for 3 miles to Temple Bruer church (GR 010 548).

The walk: Park on the green lane by the church wall and walk up the unsurfaced track with the church on your left for just over a mile. Turn right at the track junction for about 100 yards and then left up the good track with Gorse Hill Covert on your right.

After 400 yards turn left on the signposted footpath with its steep stile made with concrete blocks to follow a clearly defined path diagonally right across the field to a stile and waymark post with another footpath coming in from the left. Cross the stile and follow the headland with the wall/hedge on your immediate left to Highfield House Farm and straight on down the drive to Ermine Street or the High Dyke.

Take the path almost directly opposite straight across the field to come to the Pottergate just to the right of the house. Turn right with care round the dangerous bend and immediately left up Egg Shell Alley. Go straight on up the road to turn up Main Street to The Marquis of Granby.

After refreshment retrace your steps along Sleaford Road. Turn right along Pottergate for 350 yards and at the track junction take the signposted path diagonally left across the first field. Continue on the same line over the following fields until you come to the line of Ermine Street once again, after a mile on this cross-field path. You join the Roman road beyond Heath Farm over on the right and after the old airfield perimeter runway not far from the third machine gun post. Turn right on the road for another mile to Cocked Hat Plantation.

Do not turn left immediately at the road but turn left at the end of the plantation and straight up the track towards the church for just over a mile. *The shorter route continues* for 700 yards back to the church but *the longer route turns right* on a signposted bridleway down to the preceptory, where there is an information board.

On leaving the preceptory turn right through the farm yard down to the road and left along the road for ¾ mile, then left again up the wide, tree-lined green lane with the Warren Houses on your right. This lane takes you straight back to Temple Bruer church.

Historical Notes

Temple Bruer: Whereas the typical Lincolnshire village was founded by the Anglo-Saxons or the Danes before the Norman Conquest, Temple Bruer was first settled in 1150 by the Knights Templars, who were given land by William of Ashby (Ashby-de-la-Launde). The Templars were an order of soldier monks begun by French knights in 1118 during the first crusade to the Holy Land in order to protect pilgrims. Temple Bruer means temple or preceptory on the heath, 'bruyere' being the modern French for heathland. By 1308 Temple Bruer was the Templars' second richest property in England, largely due to sheep and wool. The Order was suppressed in England by Edward II on accusation of corruption and misconduct and by 1324 their estates were handed over to the Knights of the Hospital, or the Knights of St John, often referred to as Knights Hospitallers.

Lincoln Heath: There used to be horse racing on the Heath and the earliest Lincoln Corporation record concerning horse racing goes back to 1597. James I watched horse racing here in 1617 but the passing of the Enclosure Act in 1770 spelt the end of racing on the Heath.

Behind the church and the little school there is stabling for the ponies of children attending school.

Wellingore: The curious name of Egg Shell Alley is reputed to have come from an old lady who lived in the cottage at the end who used to put coloured egg shells in her window as decoration.

Rabbit keeping on the Heath was a major occupation, hence the Warren Houses. The usual stocking rate was five per acre and there were often 2,000 rabbits in a warren enclosed by limestone walls or walls of sod, stiffened by stakes and gorse. Segregated rabbits could be bred to produce pure pelts of black, grey or silver fur which formed the major part of their market value. The meat was the cheapest to be had which even poor labouring families could afford to buy.

The Dunston Pillar was a 'land-lighthouse' to guide people across the trackless Heath. It was originally 92 ft high and surmounted by a brazier in which a fire was lit, giving a further 15 ft in height. The Pillar was built in 1751 by Sir Francis Dashwood, Chancellor of the Exchequer 1762–63 and subsequently Lord De Despenser.

After Enclosure the course of the roads were defined and therefore there wasn't any need for a 'lighthouse' and so in 1810, Lord Hobart, the owner of the estate at that time, replaced it with a massive statue of George III to commemorate the King's 50th year on the throne. In 1941 the Air Ministry decided that the Pillar was a hazard to aircraft and perhaps a landmark for German planes and so the statue and the top third of the pillar were taken down.

Thompson's Bottom Farm is a fitting name for this slight dip in the Heath surrounded by fine trees. In 1871 the farm was 1,100 acres employing ten men and ten boys – several horsemen, a shepherd, and a garthman to look after the cattle. There were four servant girls aged 13 to 23 and two grooms. Today there is an interesting interpretative centre here which is normally open during the daylight hours from May-end to October.

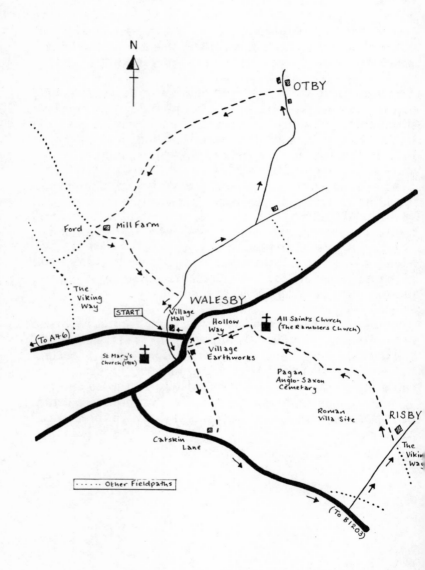

N

OTBY

Ford • Mill Farm

The Viking Way

START

Village Hall

WALESBY

Hollow Way

All Saints Church
(The Ramblers Church)

(To A46)

St Mary's Church (1914)

Village Earthworks

Pagan Anglo-Saxon Cemetery

Roman Villa Site

RISBY

The Viking Way

Catskin Lane

····· Other Fieldpaths

(To B1203)

Walesby and
The Ramblers' Church

Introduction: A surprisingly varied figure-of-eight walk with some magnificent views over the Lincolnshire Wolds that belie the belief that Lincolnshire is flat. The next parish, Normanby le Wold seen from the walk is the highest point in Lincolnshire at 548 ft above sea level. From the Armada Beacon erected at Walesby Top Church, Lincoln Cathedral may usually be seen some 18 miles away as the crow flies and even further away the cooling towers of the power stations marking the line of the river Trent.

Distance: It may be done separately in two loops of 2½ and 2 miles taking about an hour for each loop. There are two steep sections. OS Map Landranger Sheet 113 Grimsby and Cleethorpes.

Refreshments: None en route but there are two inns in neighbouring Tealby with public houses, shops and cafes in nearby Market Rasen.

How to get there: Take the A46 Lincoln to Grimsby road and then turn off the bypass into Market Rasen. Proceed through the town to turn left at the traffic lights just beyond the railway bridge on the B1203 Tealby/Binbrook road. Turn left off this road through Willingham Forest where it is signposted Walesby. Good parking at the Viking Way car park at the village hall signposted in the village (GR 133 923).

The walk: From the car park turn right uphill on Otby Lane for 1,000 yards, to turn left at the first junction along the road to Otby. About 200 yards after passing the cottage on the right and before reaching Otby House turn left down the valley through double wooden fieldgates on a signposted path.

Walk down the valley keeping the first telegraph post on the left and, after 300 yards, the fence on your right. At the bottom of the valley turn left through a metal fieldgate and then follow the hedge and stream on the right. This is the correct line of the path but an application has been made for this land to be given a Countryside Stewardship Grant, a condition of which would include unrestricted access for the public to this area.

Cross a tributary dyke by a ditchboard and shortly after a stile to follow the path across the middle of the field over marshy ground to a footbridge and waymark. Climb the embankment and walk along the dried-out mill race towards Mill Farm. Pass behind the farm and then turn left down to the ford. Cross the stream and walk up to the three-armed signpost at the edge of Mill Farm. Walk straight forward to the stile at the left of the power-line post. Cross this stile and take the left-hand path towards the hedge and walk forward to Otby Lane with the hedge on your left to turn right on the lane back to your starting place.

The second loop, starting from the car park. Turn right at the crossroads and then left up the path leading to the church. Turn left again on Rasen Lane for 200 yards and right through the signposted 'squeezer' recently made in the stone wall and into the garden. Keep to the right-hand edge of the garden with the modern house on your left (an extension was built across the correct line of the old path) to a stile. Go over the stile and across the paddock to a second stile on the left. In the field walk towards the group of trees and, after the rise, to the left of the house when it becomes visible. There is evidence here of the medieval layout of a village. Continue to the metal gate and a signpost on Catskin Lane. Turn left down the lane for 900 yards and then left up the steep drive and signposted bridleway leading to Risby Manor Farm. Almost at the top of the hill turn left off the drive over the stile onto the signposted and waymarked Viking Way footpath. Keep to the right-hand edge of the field and head for the bridge and stile in the steep valley below. Climb the hill opposite, following the waymarks to a stile in the right-hand corner by the edge of the wood. Cross the stile and walk downhill to the Ramblers' Church, looking at the Nev Cole memorial plaque and oak en route. The church is always open and it is worth a visit.

Walk down past the Armada Beacon and the hollow way to the road. Turn right for a few yards and then take the first left back to the village hall and your starting place.

Historical Notes

Nev Cole was the Area Secretary of the Lincolnshire Ramblers for over 20 years and he was one of a group of three members of the Executive who created the Viking Way 140 mile recreational path that runs from the Humber Bridge, across Lincolnshire to Oakham in Rutland, now Leicestershire. Hence the planting of a memorial oak on the Viking Way within sight of The Ramblers' Church.

The Ramblers' Church is another All Saints, which is not unusual for churches situated on ancient pre-Christian burial grounds. During excavations for a new pipeline in 1991 a pagan cemetary was uncovered on the slopes of the field between the church and the wood. The old church is 13th century and two of its eight bells were here in medieval times. It is a Grade One listed building today for the nave has massive arcades – the north side from the Norman period and the south side from the 13th century. It possesses one of the most unusual stained glass windows in the country and certainly the only one that depicts Christ mixing with a party of cyclists and ramblers. There is a thriving Friends of the Old Church Association and the ramblers have a church service here each Trinity Sunday and a Candlelight Carol

Service each December. There is only a track up to the church and in 1574 the rector left a sum of 6s 8d for the repair of this track.

Walesby is an ancient place with evidence of occupation by man from the Bronze Age onwards. A Roman villa site was explored in 1861. Walesby was the centre of the wapentake of Washcroft where the tribal elders met. There is now an Armada Beacon in the church grounds that was erected for the Fire over England celebration of the 1588 warnings of the sighting of the Spanish Armada sailing against England.

A former rector, Robert Burton (1577–1640) was the author of *The Anatomy of Melancholy*, one of the most curious works in all English literature, perhaps inspired by his remote parish.

One of the best sections of The Viking Way long distance path follows a bridleway down the hill from Normanby le Wold into Walesby, up the church track and then on along the ridge to Risby and the lovely village of Tealby with its Tennyson connections.